The Gospel of Matthew

Ben Witherington III

Cover design by Strange Last Name
Page layout by PerfecType, Nashville, Tennessee

Witherington, Ben, III, 1951-.
The Gospel of Matthew / Ben Witherington, III. – Franklin, Tennessee : Seedbed Publishing, ©2018.

pages ; cm. + 1 videodisc – (OneBook. Daily-weekly)

ISBN 9781628240627 (paperback)
ISBN 9781628245714 (DVD)
ISBN 9781628240634 (Mobi)
ISBN 9781628240641 (ePub)
ISBN 9781628240658 (uPDF)

1. Bible. Matthew -- Textbooks. 2. Bible. Matthew -- Study and teaching.
3. Bible. Matthew -- Commentaries. I. Title. II. Series.

BS2575.6.W57 20183   226.2/07   2018961996

 Seedbed

SEEDBED PUBLISHING
Franklin, Tennessee
seedbed.com

CONTENTS

Contents

Contents

Week Eight
The Passion and Resurrection of the Christ

Wesleyan Quadrilateral

* Scripture
  Tradition
  Reason
  Experience

WELCOME TO ONEBOOK DAILY-WEEKLY

John Wesley, in a letter to one of his leaders, penned the following:

> O begin! Fix some part of every day for private exercises. You may acquire the taste which you have not: what is tedious at first, will afterwards be pleasant. Whether you like it or not, read and pray daily. It is for your life; there is no other way; else you will be a trifler all your days. . . . Do justice to your own soul; give it time and means to grow. Do not starve yourself any longer. Take up your cross and be a Christian altogether.

Rarely are our lives most shaped by our biggest ambitions and highest aspirations. Rather, our lives are most shaped, for better or for worse, by those small things we do every single day.

At Seedbed, our biggest ambition and highest aspiration is to resource the followers of Jesus to become lovers and doers of the Word of God every single day, to become people of One Book.

To that end, we have created the OneBook Daily-Weekly. First, it's important to understand what this is not: warm, fuzzy, sentimental devotions. If you engage the Daily-Weekly for any length of time, you will learn the Word of God. You will grow profoundly in your love for God, and you will become a passionate lover of people.

How Does the Daily-Weekly Work?

Daily. As the name implies, every day invites a short but substantive engagement with the Bible. Five days a week you will read a passage of scripture followed by a short segment of teaching and closing with questions for reflection and self-examination. On the sixth day, you will review and reflect on the previous five days.

Weekly. Each week, on the seventh day, find a way to gather with at least one other person doing the study. Pursue the weekly guidance for gathering. Share learning, insight, encouragement, and most important, how the Holy Spirit is working in your lives.

That's it. Depending on the length of the study, when the eight or twelve weeks are done, we will be ready with the next study. On an ongoing basis, we will release new editions of the Daily-Weekly. Over time, those who pursue this course of learning will develop a rich library of Bible learning resources for the long haul.

OneBook Daily-Weekly will develop eight- and twelve-week studies that cover the entire Old and New Testaments. Seedbed will publish new studies regularly so that an ongoing supply of group lessons will be available. All titles will remain accessible, which means they can be used in any order that fits your needs or the needs of your group.

If you are looking for a substantive study to learn scripture through a steadfast method, look no further.

WEEK ONE

Matthew 1–4

You Shall Call Him Immanuel*

ONE

Introduction

Key Observation. This Gospel's distinctive portrait of Jesus focuses on Jesus as God's Wisdom come in person (Immanuel) and as a wise teacher.

Understanding the Word. The Gospel of Matthew was the most popular of the four Gospels in the first few centuries of Christianity. It was written for Jewish Christians who were familiar with the Old Testament and especially with Jewish Wisdom Literature (for example, Proverbs, Ecclesiastes, Wisdom of Solomon, Sirach). The First Evangelist seeks to present Jesus as both a wise man and as God's wisdom incarnate, God come in person to his people, Immanuel (which means "God with us"). Thus, we have six blocks of teaching in this Gospel, beginning with Matthew 5–7, which depict Jesus as one even greater than Moses or Solomon, whose teaching is the definitive revelation of God's will for his people. Not surprisingly, it was this Gospel that was used repeatedly in the early church for discipling new Christians, teaching them what they should believe, how they should behave, and how to practice their faith in terms of prayer, fasting and feasting, almsgiving, worship, and much more.

This Gospel was written in the form of an ancient biography, which did not have the same form as modern biographies. For one thing, sheer limitations of

---

*For those wanting much more on this Gospel, see Ben Witherington III, *Matthew* (Macon, GA: Smyth & Helwys, 2006).

length meant that it had to be much more selective in the material it included. The ancients believed that a person was born with a certain personality and that while it was revealed over time, it was not developed over time. Thus, there was no need to focus on someone's youth or growth into adulthood. In short, it was an adult-oriented culture.

Just as the origins of a person were believed to reveal much about who a person was, so also it was believed that how a person died most revealed their character. In the case of Jesus, this was problematic since he died in the most shameful way imaginable in antiquity—on a Roman cross. It is for this reason that the Gospel writers spend about one-third of their total account on the last week of Jesus' life. This shocking end to the life of a person who had been admired by many for his teaching and miracles had to be explained in detail, and for Jewish Christians, it had to be explained in terms of scripture, showing that it was part of God's plan all along.

Scholars are divided over whether Matthew was a source for this Gospel (perhaps its unique material, perhaps also its collection of six blocks of teaching material) or the final author/editor. In either case, the Gospel reflects a person like Matthew the tax collector, who indeed would have been literate and presumably able to organize source material quite readily.

The structure of the Gospel, which, broadly speaking, follows a chronological outline (birth, baptism, temptation and ministry, climactic final week of life, resurrection, and appearances to disciples), also alternates between the actions of Jesus and the teachings of Jesus. In other words, the Evangelist himself has organized the material in this way within the larger framework of the ministry of Jesus. This was not unusual in an ancient biography. Following a strict chronology of events and activities was not required. The main thing was to be selective and include that material that best revealed the character of the person about whom the biography was written.

1. What features of Matthew's Gospel made it popular from the early church until today? *teaches Christians how to practice their faith*

2. Why do all the Gospel writers, and Matthew in particular, spend so little time on Jesus' birth and early life and focus so heavily on his final days? *At that time, it was believed that how a person died reflected their character.*

TWO

Ancestry and Divine Origins

Matthew 1:1–25 ESV *The book of the genealogy of Jesus Christ, the son of David, the son of Abraham.*

²Abraham was the father of Isaac, and Isaac the father of Jacob, and Jacob the father of Judah and his brothers, ³and Judah the father of Perez and Zerah by Tamar, and Perez the father of Hezron, and Hezron the father of Ram, ⁴and Ram the father of Amminadab, and Amminadab the father of Nahshon, and Nahshon the father of Salmon, ⁵and Salmon the father of Boaz by Rahab, and Boaz the father of Obed by Ruth, and Obed the father of Jesse, ⁶and Jesse the father of David the king.

And David was the father of Solomon by the wife of Uriah, ⁷and Solomon the father of Rehoboam, and Rehoboam the father of Abijah, and Abijah the father of Asaph, ⁸and Asaph the father of Jehoshaphat, and Jehoshaphat the father of Joram, and Joram the father of Uzziah, ⁹and Uzziah the father of Jotham, and Jotham the father of Ahaz, and Ahaz the father of Hezekiah, ¹⁰and Hezekiah the father of Manasseh, and Manasseh the father of Amos, and Amos the father of Josiah, ¹¹and Josiah the father of Jechoniah and his brothers, at the time of the deportation to Babylon.

¹²And after the deportation to Babylon: Jechoniah was the father of Shealtiel, and Shealtiel the father of Zerubbabel, ¹³and Zerubbabel the father of Abiud, and Abiud the father of Eliakim, and Eliakim the father of Azor, ¹⁴and Azor the father of Zadok, and Zadok the father of Achim, and Achim the father of Eliud, ¹⁵and Eliud the father of Eleazar, and Eleazar the father of Matthan, and Matthan the father of Jacob, ¹⁶and Jacob the father of Joseph the husband of Mary, of whom Jesus was born, who is called Christ.

¹⁷So all the generations from Abraham to David were fourteen generations, and from David to the deportation to Babylon fourteen generations, and from the deportation to Babylon to the Christ fourteen generations.

¹⁸Now the birth of Jesus Christ took place in this way. When his mother Mary had been betrothed to Joseph, before they came together she was found to be with child from the Holy Spirit. ¹⁹And her husband Joseph, being a just man and unwilling to put her to shame, resolved to divorce her quietly. ²⁰But as he considered these things, behold, an angel of the Lord appeared to him in a dream, saying, "Joseph, son of David, do not fear to take Mary as your wife, for that which is conceived in her is from the Holy Spirit. ²¹She will bear a son, and you shall call his name Jesus, for he will save his people from their sins." ²²All this took place to fulfill what the Lord had spoken by the prophet: ²³"Behold, the virgin shall conceive and bear a son, and they shall call his name Immanuel" (which means, God with us). ²⁴When Joseph woke from sleep, he did as the angel of the Lord commanded him: he took his wife, ²⁵but knew her not until she had given birth to a son. And he called his name Jesus.

Key Observation. While human ancestry matters, what matters more is being born of God.

Understanding the Word. Without question, the genealogy in Matthew 1 is one of the strangest genealogies you'll encounter. First, this is Joseph's genealogy rather than Mary's. Yet, Joseph had exactly nothing to do with the conception of Jesus—he was conceived by the Holy Spirit. So why do we have Joseph's genealogy here, and how is it that Jesus is a "son of David"? The answer comes from studying the historical context. In early Judaism, if a Jewish man adopted a child, he was not only entitled to whatever inheritance his father left him in a will, he was entitled to claim his stepfather's ancestry too!

Second, this is a male genealogy, but there are some women included! This was unusual in an ancient patriarchal culture. These women all had irregularities in their story, to say the least. Tamar, the wife of Judah, was actually a Canaanite. Rahab was a woman who ran a bordello in Jericho and was also not a Hebrew. Ruth, like Rahab, was non-Jewish—she was a Moabitess who became the wife of Boaz. Uriah's wife (a.k.a. Bathsheba) was only David's wife through an act of adultery, and she had previously been married to a Hittite. What these women all share in common are irregular unions with Jewish men. Had our writer wanted to emphasize miraculous conceptions, he might have mentioned Sarah, Rebekah, and Rachel, but he did not. I suspect that our author includes these women in the genealogy to indicate something about the irregular or out-of-the-ordinary ways God fulfills his mission. If God can use even these women and these means to create the lineage of the Jewish Messiah, then the divine irregularity in Mary's life in regard to the conception of Jesus shouldn't come as a total shock. What might seem scandalous from a pious human point of view was not scandalous from God's point of view.

Third, the genealogy is incomplete. In other words, it leaves not only individual names out, as a careful study of Old Testament genealogies would show, but whole generations, especially toward the latter part of the genealogy. As it turns out, this genealogy is not like the kind you might come up with by consulting www.ancestry.com. In fact, especially with royal genealogies, it was not unusual to schematize the whole of it, and leave out some of the less honorable skeletons in the closet. Matthew does not so much do that (otherwise, why mention Rahab?) as he is keen to make clear that Jesus is the seventh son of the seventh son of King David. Seven, in early Jewish ways of thinking, was the number of perfection, and so the whole point of the form of the genealogy was to make clear that Jesus was the perfect king, the perfect heir of King David, the true and genuine Messiah. While this sort of selective and scandalous genealogy might seem odd to us, it would convincingly make the theological points Matthew wants to make with his Jewish Christian audience.

We now shift to Matthew 1:18–25. According to Jewish customs, a couple would become engaged and legally married for a full year before the wedding ceremony and the consummation of the marriage. Thus, we should not be surprised when we hear about Joseph resolving to *divorce* his fiancée. They had already gone through the first legal portion of the marriage contract. So it was a true shock for Joseph to discover Mary's pregnancy before the consummation of the marriage. Young Jewish women were absolutely expected to be virgins prior to the consummation of the marriage. To not be a virgin was considered very shameful. Jewish girls were usually engaged just after puberty, so at an age of twelve or thirteen. The men, who came to puberty a bit later, would be a bit older.

Matthew cites Isaiah 7:14 in order to indicate that this divine irregularity was part of God's plan, but we need to understand that early Jews did not read Isaiah 7:14 as a reference to a miraculous conception in a virgin's womb. The Hebrew simply says, "a young nubile woman of marriageable age will conceive." The Greek translation of that verse, however, uses the word *parthenos* ("virgin"), which places special emphasis on the woman's virginity, something which is only implied by the Hebrew. My point is that it is not that prophecy that led to the making up of a fictitious story about a virginal conception. No, it was the actual shocking event in Mary's life, the unexpected miracle, that led later Christian writers like Matthew to search the Scriptures to see if such a thing had been foretold.

Matthew 1:25 reports that Joseph did not know her until after she conceived and gave birth to Jesus. This implies that he went on to have normal sexual relationships with Mary thereafter, and thus explains later references to Jesus' brothers and sisters. Since the miracle occurred at conception and not at Jesus' birth, we should speak of the virginal conception, not the virgin birth.

Joseph named the child "Jesus," which means "Yahweh saves." In that culture, names were meant to connote something about the nature or origins of the person. This raises the expectation of Jesus' identity as we begin his story.

1. What is odd about the genealogy in Matthew 1, and how do we explain its peculiar features? *Complete, including skeleton 7th son of 7th son*
2. Why was it important for Jesus to be born of a virgin? *Proof that he was a diety*

THREE

Wise Men Still Seek Him

Matthew 2:1–23 ESV *Now after Jesus was born in Bethlehem of Judea in the days of Herod the king, behold, wise men from the east came to Jerusalem, ²saying, "Where is he who has been born king of the Jews? For we saw his star when it rose and have come to worship him." ³When Herod the king heard this, he was troubled, and all Jerusalem with him; ⁴and assembling all the chief priests and scribes of the people, he inquired of them where the Christ was to be born. ⁵They told him, "In Bethlehem of Judea, for so it is written by the prophet: ⁶'And you, O Bethlehem, in the land of Judah, are by no means least among the rulers of Judah; for from you shall come a ruler who will shepherd my people Israel.'"*

⁷Then Herod summoned the wise men secretly and ascertained from them what time the star had appeared. ⁸And he sent them to Bethlehem, saying, "Go and search diligently for the child, and when you have found him, bring me word, that I too may come and worship him." ⁹After listening to the king, they went on their way. And behold, the star that they had seen when it rose went before them until it came to rest over the place where the child was. ¹⁰When they saw the star, they rejoiced exceedingly with great joy. ¹¹And going into the house, they saw the child with Mary his mother, and they fell down and worshiped him. Then, opening their treasures, they offered him gifts, gold and frankincense and myrrh. [12]And being warned in a dream not to return to Herod, they departed to their own country by another way.

[13]Now when they had departed, behold, an angel of the Lord appeared to Joseph in a dream and said, "Rise, take the child and his mother, and flee to Egypt, and remain there until I tell you, for Herod is about to search for the child, to destroy him." [14]And he rose and took the child and his mother by night and departed to Egypt [15]and remained there until the death of Herod. This was to fulfill what the Lord had spoken by the prophet, "Out of Egypt I called my son."

[16]Then Herod, when he saw that he had been tricked by the wise men, became furious, and he sent and killed all the male children in Bethlehem and in all that region who were two years old or under, according to the time that he had ascertained from the wise men. [17]Then was fulfilled what was spoken by the prophet Jeremiah: [18]"A voice was heard in Ramah, weeping and loud lamentation, Rachel weeping for her children; she refused to be comforted, because they are no more."

[19]But when Herod died, behold, an angel of the Lord appeared in a dream to Joseph in Egypt, [20]saying, "Rise, take the child and his mother and go to the land of Israel, for those who sought the child's life are dead." [21]And he rose and took the child and his mother and went to the land of Israel. [22]But when he heard that Archelaus was reigning over Judea in place of his father Herod, he was afraid to go there, and being warned in a dream he withdrew to the district of Galilee. [23]And he went and lived in a city called Nazareth, so that what was spoken by the prophets might be fulfilled, that he would be called a Nazarene.

Key Observation. The traditional Christmas story needs an extreme makeover if it is to be in agreement with what Matthew and Luke actually say happened.

Understanding the Word. Matthew 1–2 and Luke 1–2 come at the story of Jesus' origins from different angles, with Luke focusing more on the story of Mary, and Matthew focusing more on Joseph. One of the problems with our over familiarity with the Christmas story is that we tend to blend together in our minds Luke 1–2 and Matthew 1–2. It is important that we allow Matthew's account to speak for itself.

When Jesus was born in Bethlehem, the ruler of Judea was Herod the Great. He was only partially Jewish. He also was Idumean, which is to say from Edom, the sworn enemy of Israel in antiquity. He was a ruthless dictator who had won the kingship by force. Herod built fortresses for his protection and even executed members of his own family whose existence threated his reign. These facts make it clear that the slaughter of the innocents was totally possible given his reputation. Additionally, Herod died somewhere between 4 and 2 BC. This means that Jesus was actually born somewhere between 6 and 4 BC while Herod was still alive.

This narrative introduces us to astrologers, possibly from Persia. Unlike modern astrology, the ancients actually believed the stars were beings, the heavenly host, moving across the sky foreshadowing things to come. Here the astrologers are quite properly called magi, a word from which we get the word "magician." They were not kings, though they often served kings. Nor were there necessarily three magi. This number comes from their three kinds of gifts. They were looking for the birth of a miracle child. These events happen after the birth of Jesus as Herod is killing sons.

When the magi locate Jesus, Mary and Joseph are at home, which is to say, in a house, not in a barn and not in a cave. Since Joseph had relatives in Bethlehem, they probably stayed in the family home with relatives.

The prophecy about a birth of the Messiah in Bethlehem comes from Micah 5:2, but the wise men do not know this prophecy until Herod consults with the priests and scholars. Both Herod and Jerusalem are disturbed by this revelation and caught unaware. There is some irony that foreigners are more spiritually in tune with God's plan than the current ruler and his Jewish counselors in Jerusalem.

Herod tells the wise men to go and find the child and come back and give him a report so "that I too may come and worship him" (v. 8). But the wise men are told in a dream that this was not Herod's true intention, so they secretly slip away back to their homeland. But before doing that, they bring expensive gifts to the miracle child—gifts of gold, frankincense, and myrrh. These luxury items were fit for a king.

The means of divine communication in several cases in Matthew 1–2 is by dreams: (1) Joseph is told in a dream it is all right to take Mary as his wife; (2) the wise men are warned in a dream not to return to Herod; (3) Joseph is warned in a dream to get out of the country quickly; and, finally, (4) Joseph is warned in two dreams to return to Israel from Egypt but to avoid Judea because Herod's son Archelaus was now the ruler. Matthew 1–2 are stories full of unexpected twists and turns and surprises. Matthew is suggesting that while God's Word provides some guidance, God intervenes in dreams to convey direction and help when immediate assistance is required.

The story concludes by telling us that the holy family goes to Nazareth, and that this, too, is in fulfillment of prophecy, though we are unsure which prophecy Matthew had in mind in this case. Was Jesus like the prophet Samuel who had taken a Nazaritie vow (see 1 Samuel 1:11; cf. Numbers 6:1–21)? More certainly, there seems to have been a connection between Bethlehem and Nazareth, for the city's name means "branch town" (*netzerit*), and this is likely a metaphorical allusion to the branch or shoot of Jesse, which is to say the Messiah. In other words, it would appear that some Davidic folk had settled in Nazareth, who ultimately were from Bethlehem, hence the connection for Joseph and others between these two towns.

1. What do you make of the revelations in dreams to Joseph and the wise men in these stories? Have you ever had a dream that came true or revealed a key truth you had previously not known?

2. From the start of the story, Jesus' life seems marked by danger and even possible scandal. Since this was true for Jesus, how should we evaluate the trials and tribulations in our own lives?

FOUR

John the Baptizer and Jesus' First Public Appearance

Matthew 3:1–17 *In those days John the Baptist came, preaching in the wilderness of Judea ²and saying, "Repent, for the kingdom of heaven has come near." ³This is he who was spoken of through the prophet Isaiah: "A voice of one calling in the wilderness, 'Prepare the way for the Lord, make straight paths for him.'"*

⁴John's clothes were made of camel's hair, and he had a leather belt around his waist. His food was locusts and wild honey. ⁵People went out to him from

Jerusalem and all Judea and the whole region of the Jordan. ⁶*Confessing their sins, they were baptized by him in the Jordan River.*

⁷*But when he saw many of the Pharisees and Sadducees coming to where he was baptizing, he said to them: "You brood of vipers! Who warned you to flee from the coming wrath?* ⁸*Produce fruit in keeping with repentance.* ⁹*And do not think you can say to yourselves, 'We have Abraham as our father.' I tell you that out of these stones God can raise up children for Abraham.* ¹⁰*The ax is already at the root of the trees, and every tree that does not produce good fruit will be cut down and thrown into the fire.*

¹¹*"I baptize you with water for repentance. But after me comes one who is more powerful than I, whose sandals I am not worthy to carry. He will baptize you with the Holy Spirit and fire.* ¹²*His winnowing fork is in his hand, and he will clear his threshing floor, gathering his wheat into the barn and burning up the chaff with unquenchable fire."*

¹³*Then Jesus came from Galilee to the Jordan to be baptized by John.* ¹⁴*But John tried to deter him, saying, "I need to be baptized by you, and do you come to me?"*

¹⁵*Jesus replied, "Let it be so now; it is proper for us to do this to fulfill all righteousness." Then John consented.*

¹⁶*As soon as Jesus was baptized, he went up out of the water. At that moment heaven was opened, and he saw the Spirit of God descending like a dove and alighting on him.* ¹⁷*And a voice from heaven said, "This is my Son, whom I love; with him I am well pleased."*

Key Observation. A private revelation to Jesus of his unique identity in Mark's Gospel becomes a public declaration of that identity in Matthew at Jesus' baptism.

Understanding the Word. All four Gospels introduce John the Baptizer as the forerunner of Jesus, the one who prepares the way for the Jewish Messiah. Matthew, Mark, and Luke emphasize this by associating John with a prophecy from Isaiah 40:3: "A voice of one calling: 'In the wilderness prepare the way for the LORD; make straight in the desert a highway for our God.'" This prophecy refers to a path being made in the desert. The original image was of God himself leading his people back from Babylonian exile and a herald going before God and speaking about the making of a road for that mass exodus from Babylon. John in Matthew 3 is seen as that herald, and Jesus as that divine figure.

John is depicted as a prophet like Elijah in his garb, and perhaps in his lifestyle as well (cf. 2 Kings 1:8 and Zechariah 13:4). But it is Jesus, not John, who performs miracles like Elijah on Elijah's old turf, Galilee. And it is clear that there was confusion among the people—was John the Elijah-like figure who would prepare the way for the coming day of Yahweh, as Malachi 4:5–6 at the very end of the Old Testament predicted, or was Jesus the Elijah figure (see Matthew 16:14 when people were saying Jesus was John back from the dead or Elijah)? In any case, John is famous for his water ritual, baptizing people in the Jordan and calling them to repentance before God's judgment falls upon them.

It is instructive to compare Mark 1:1–11 to Matthew 3. In Mark's portrayal of the event, which Matthew uses as a source for his rendition, Mark depicts the revelation at the river as a private disclosure to Jesus himself, though the baptism itself is a public event in both texts. Mark is portraying the event as Jesus having an apocalyptic vision at the river. Jesus sees the sky crack open and the Spirit descending like a dove on him, and only Jesus hears a voice saying, "You are my Son, whom I love; with you I am well pleased" (v. 11). Then the Spirit drives Jesus out into the wilderness. In Matthew, however, we have a public announcement: "This is my Son" (v. 17), which concludes the story. And then, in Matthew 4:1, the Spirit leads, not drives, Jesus into the wilderness. Matthew makes this the first public announcement of Jesus' ministry.

Both Matthew and Mark describe John as a preacher of repentance (Matt. 3:1; Mark 1:1–5). The description of John's garb and food is basically the same in both accounts. Mark does not have the condemnation of the Pharisees and Sadducees at the river, nor the remark that they are called a brood of vipers who need to repent. This is just in Matthew's account. Both accounts tell us that John speaks of one coming after him whose sandals he is unworthy to untie, and they also both say that while John baptized with water, the Coming One would baptize with the Spirit (and Matthew adds "and fire"). There is nothing in Mark about axes laid to roots or winnowing of grain or clearing a threshing floor. Matthew clearly has the more public and also the more dramatic depiction of the wrath to come envisioned by John.

There is also one more important element to the story that is not in Mark but is added by Matthew. Why does John attempt to deter Jesus from baptism? Jesus' baptism is said "to fulfill all righteousness," but what does that mean?

John doesn't think Jesus needs a baptism of repentance, but he himself does. Probably we are meant to think that Jesus is taking on the role of lost Israel here, who does indeed need to be cleansed. Jesus is Israel gone right, and fulfilling all righteousness for Israel. But he is also much more than that—he is announced by God as his beloved Son on the same occasion.

1. What do you make of Jesus' relationship with John in Matthew's account?

2. Why did Jesus allow himself to be baptized with John's repentance baptism?

FIVE

Attempting to Overcome a Tempting

Matthew 4:1–25 *Then Jesus was led by the Spirit into the wilderness to be tempted by the devil. ²After fasting forty days and forty nights, he was hungry. ³The tempter came to him and said, "If you are the Son of God, tell these stones to become bread."*

⁴Jesus answered, "It is written: 'Man shall not live on bread alone, but on every word that comes from the mouth of God.'"

⁵Then the devil took him to the holy city and had him stand on the highest point of the temple. ⁶"If you are the Son of God," he said, "throw yourself down. For it is written: "'He will command his angels concerning you, and they will lift you up in their hands, so that you will not strike your foot against a stone.'"

⁷Jesus answered him, "It is also written: 'Do not put the Lord your God to the test.'"

⁸Again, the devil took him to a very high mountain and showed him all the kingdoms of the world and their splendor. ⁹"All this I will give you," he said, "if you will bow down and worship me."

¹⁰Jesus said to him, "Away from me, Satan! For it is written: 'Worship the Lord your God, and serve him only.'"

¹¹Then the devil left him, and angels came and attended him.

¹²When Jesus heard that John had been put in prison, he withdrew to Galilee. ¹³Leaving Nazareth, he went and lived in Capernaum, which was by the lake in the area of Zebulun and Naphtali—[14]to fulfill what was said through the prophet Isaiah: [15]"Land of Zebulun and land of Naphtali, the Way of the Sea, beyond the Jordan, Galilee of the Gentiles—[16]the people living in darkness have seen a great light; on those living in the land of the shadow of death a light has dawned."

[17]From that time on Jesus began to preach, "Repent, for the kingdom of heaven has come near."

[18]As Jesus was walking beside the Sea of Galilee, he saw two brothers, Simon called Peter and his brother Andrew. They were casting a net into the lake, for they were fishermen. [19]"Come, follow me," Jesus said, "and I will send you out to fish for people." [20]At once they left their nets and followed him.

[21]Going on from there, he saw two other brothers, James son of Zebedee and his brother John. They were in a boat with their father Zebedee, preparing their nets. Jesus called them,[22]and immediately they left the boat and their father and followed him.

[23]Jesus went throughout Galilee, teaching in their synagogues, proclaiming the good news of the kingdom, and healing every disease and sickness among the people. [24]News about him spread all over Syria, and people brought to him all who were ill with various diseases, those suffering severe pain, the demon-possessed, those having seizures, and the paralyzed; and he healed them. [25]Large crowds from Galilee, the Decapolis, Jerusalem, Judea and the region across the Jordan followed him.

Key Observation. Jesus is depicted as both human and divine right from the outset of his ministry.

Understanding the Word. The prelude to Jesus' ministry is the story of his wilderness temptation. There are several important keys to understanding this story: (1) Jesus is being tempted as the divine Son of God, one who is both divine and human; (2) when the Son of God took on a human nature, he had to accept the normal limitations of human beings—limitations of time, space, knowledge, power, and mortality; (3) when Jesus was tempted, he could have called on his divine nature to deal with the problem, but instead he chose to use the two resources we all have to use to deal with temptations and problems—the Word of God and the Spirit of God; and (4) the word *peirasmos* can refer to either a tempting or a testing. Basically, a temptation is Satan's attempt to destroy someone's character, whereas a test from God is an attempt to strengthen someone's good character. For this reason, when we get to the Lord's Prayer in Matthew 6:13 we should read it: "Do not put us to the test, but rather deliver us from the Evil One." This is probably a prayer that Jesus himself, in fact, was praying while dealing with his trial in the wilderness. God tempts no one and cannot be tempted (James 1:13)!

The three temptations increase in severity—a temptation to satisfy one's hunger when one has been fasting for forty days, a temptation to demonstrate his divine identity by throwing himself off the pinnacle of the temple in Jerusalem and commanding angels to catch him, and finally a temptation to worship the Dark Lord, the Devil, and thereby achieve the good end of world rulership by Jesus, by entirely the wrong means. Jesus responds by citing Deuteronomy 8:3, 6:16, and 6:13. Satan meanwhile was able to quote only a snippet of a song—Psalm 91:11–12. From a Jewish point of view, the Law had far more authority and clout than one of the songs in the Psalter, and so Satan loses the Scripture battle and his prey slips through his fingers.

According to both Mark and Matthew, Jesus' ministry doesn't really begin in earnest until after John has been arrested by Herod Antipas, and also after Jesus' baptism and temptation. In Matthew, the break with the past seems very clear because Jesus leaves his home in Nazareth and makes Capernaum by the sea his home base for his ministry (Matthew 4:13). Matthew punctuates this by quoting Isaiah 9:1–2. Jesus then proclaims initially a message much the same as John's—repent for the kingdom of God is at hand (cf. Matthew 3:2; 4:17). Matthew, however, prefers the word "heaven" to the word "God" in this phrase, though he is talking about the very same thing—the inbreaking of God's final saving activity in the ministry of Jesus. Jews like our Evangelist sought to avoid misusing the sacred name of God by using "heaven" as an indirect reference.

The Greek word *baseleia*, too often translated "kingdom," requires some comment. In English, the word "kingdom" is a noun that always connotes a place. But the Greek word *baseleia* and the Aramaic word *malkuta* sometimes have a verbal sense referring to an activity and sometimes have a noun sense. Whenever Jesus uses this word in the present tense, he is not referring to a place, he is referring to an activity. But when he is speaking of it in a future tense, and talks about inheriting or entering the *baseleia/malkuta,* he does indeed mean a place, a place he tells the disciples will one day come on earth as it already is in heaven. In short, the word should be translated "dominion" because in English one can have dominion over someone (verbal sense), or enter a dominion (noun sense). So when Jesus says "repent for the dominion is at hand," he means the final divine saving activity has just invaded your space and you'd better repent!

In Matthew 4:18–22, Jesus calls four fishermen to become disciples (*mathetes* means "learners"). These are two pairs of brothers, Simon and Andrew, and the Zebedee brothers, James and John. From the outset, Jesus announces to these fishermen that they will still be fishing, if they follow him, only they will be fishing for followers, for human beings.

According to the summary at the end of the chapter in Matthew 4:23–25, Jesus quickly gains a reputation as a teacher, preacher, and especially as a healer, for people were bringing the sick and impaired to him from all over the region—not just Galilee, but also from Syria and the Decapolis, the Greek cities which surrounded Galilee. Thus, the chapter ends describing the huge crowds Jesus was drawing, but as Matthew will emphasize, Jesus' main ministry was teaching and preaching the good news of salvation. Healing the body was good, but giving a person the gift of everlasting life was far more important, and Jesus concentrated on the latter. His main mission was to let people know that God's final saving activity was now happening—through him. He did this through his words and deeds.

1. How do Jesus' temptations provide a model for dealing with temptation in our lives?

2. What were Jesus' priorities in his ministry?

WEEK ONE

GATHERING DISCUSSION OUTLINE

A. Open session in prayer. Ask that God would astonish us anew with fresh insight from his Word and transform us into the disciples that Jesus desires us to become.

B. View video for this week's readings.

C. What were key insights or takeaways that you gained from your reading during the week and from watching the video commentary? In particular, how did these help you to grow in your faith and understanding of Scripture? What parts of the Bible lesson or study raised questions for you?

D. Discuss questions selected from the daily readings.

1. **KEY OBSERVATION:** This Gospel's distinctive portrait of Jesus focuses on Jesus as God's Wisdom come in person (Immanuel) and as a wise teacher.

DISCUSSION QUESTION: Why do all the Gospel writers, and Matthew in particular, spend so little time on Jesus' birth and early life and focus so heavily on his final days?

2. **KEY OBSERVATION:** While human ancestry matters, what matters more is being born of God.

DISCUSSION QUESTION: What is odd about the genealogy in Matthew 1, and how do we explain its peculiar features?

3. **KEY OBSERVATION:** The traditional Christmas story needs an extreme makeover if it is to be in agreement with what Matthew and Luke actually say happened.

   DISCUSSION QUESTION: From the start of the story, Jesus' life seems marked by danger and even possible scandal. Since this was true for Jesus, how should we evaluate the trials and tribulations in our own lives?

4. **KEY OBSERVATION:** A private revelation to Jesus of his unique identity in Mark's Gospel becomes a public declaration of that identity in Matthew at Jesus' baptism.

   DISCUSSION QUESTION: Why did Jesus allow himself to be baptized with John's repentance baptism?

5. **KEY OBSERVATION:** Jesus is depicted as both human and divine right from the outset of his ministry.

   DISCUSSION QUESTION: How do Jesus' temptations provide a model for dealing with temptation in our lives?

E. As the study concludes, consider specific ways that this week's Bible lesson invites us to grow and calls us to change. How do this week's scriptures call us to think differently? How do they challenge us to change in order to align ourselves with God's work in the world? What specific actions should we take to apply the insights of the lesson into our daily lives? What kind of person does our Bible lesson call us to become?

F. Close session with prayer. Emphasize God's ongoing work of transformation in our lives in preparation for loving mission and service in the world. Pray for missing class members as well as for persons whom we need to invite to join our study.

Matthew 5–7

The Sermon on the Mount

ONE

Surveying the Sermon

Key Observation. The Sermon on the Mount is a collection of Jesus' core teachings on how his followers should live.

Understanding the Word. There are several keys to understanding Matthew 5–7. First, one needs to realize that Jesus is presenting his ethics in a framework deeply influenced by the Wisdom Literature of the Old Testament—Proverbs, Ecclesiastes, and the Psalms. The second important point is that Jesus is bringing in the saving reign of God, what we call the kingdom. So these are ethics in light of the inbreaking kingdom, not merely a reflection on some aspects of the Mosaic law or prophetic law or ethics. The new eschatological situation means that new and more demanding imperatives will be offered by Jesus. For example, Moses says no adultery. Jesus says there should not even be any adulterous thoughts. Clearly, this intensification of the demand is only possible if God's saving activity is changing human hearts and behavior. Third, this is ethics for disciples. It was never meant to be imposed on society in general. One must first be a disciple before these sorts of demands become expectations.

Matthew 5–7 begins with kingdom beatitudes ("blessings") and ends with a parable about living wisely. In other words, it begins with what God will do or is doing for the disciples, and ends with how one can live wisely in light of life's uncertainties, including our mortality. Along the way, Jesus talks about fulfilling the Law and the Prophets. Notice that he doesn't just mention the

Law, but also the Prophets. And, more important, the language of "fulfill-ment" indicates that the last days have arrived, the time when God's promises and prophecies finally come to fruition. Fulfillment is one thing, obedience is another. Jesus is not calling for doubling down on one's obedience to the Mosaic covenant; he is saying that in the new eschatological situation, and in view of the new saving activity of God, the ultimate aims of the Law and the Prophets are being fulfilled—namely, that God's people love God with their whole hearts and their neighbors as themselves, and even love their enemies, living lives of righteousness and integrity and holiness, by the grace and saving empowerment of God. The Sermon on the Mount is not a utopian ethic. If it were merely up to a disciple, he could never live up to these demands on his own. But the premise is that God is now enabling his people to do what he demands; indeed, even do more than what Moses had previously demanded. This ethic is as much a statement of what God can do in the believer as a state-ment of what God expects the believer to do. God gives what he commands. It is not an accident that prayer, specifically the Lord's Prayer, is at the center of this sermon. Constant reliance on God is required if one is going to behave in these ways. And finally, this sermon provides something of a character state-ment about Jesus and his own behavior—he calls his disciples to take up their crosses and follow him, emulating his behavior. This includes radical things like being chaste, and not only avoiding all violence, but, in fact, loving one's enemy and praying for one's persecutors.

1. What is the character of the Sermon on the Mount? Is it law? Utopian ethic? Wisdom?

2. Does the Sermon on the Mount simply make radical demands on disciples, or does it provide clues as to how one can live into these commands with God's help?

TWO

The Beatitudes

Matthew 5:3–12 *"Blessed are the poor in spirit, for theirs is the kingdom of heaven. ⁴Blessed are those who mourn, for they will be comforted. ⁵Blessed are* *the meek, for they will inherit the earth. ⁶Blessed are those who hunger and thirst for righteousness, for they will be filled. ⁷Blessed are the merciful, for they will be shown mercy. ⁸Blessed are the pure in heart, for they will see God. ⁹Blessed are the peacemakers, for they will be called children of God. ¹⁰Blessed are those who are persecuted because of righteousness, for theirs is the kingdom of heaven.*

¹¹"Blessed are you when people insult you, persecute you and falsely say all kinds of evil against you because of me. ¹²Rejoice and be glad, because great is your reward in heaven, for in the same way they persecuted the prophets who were before you."

Key Observation. The Beatitudes are, in fact, not primarily about our human attitudes, rather they are about the various ways God will bless his people who are poor in spirit, mourning, meek, hungering for a more righteous world, merciful, pure in heart, peacemakers, persecuted, and insulted. In short, God will bless those who behave in Christlike ways.

Understanding the Word. The first and, in some ways, most important thing to note about these nine blessings is that the payoff comes later—the kingdom already belongs to the disciple, but it has not yet fully come (hence "thy kingdom come" in the Lord's Prayer). *In the future,* the mourning will be comforted, the meek will inherit the earth, those who hunger for a righteous world will be satisfied, the pure in heart who long for God will find their heart's desire, the peacemakers will be recognized as God's children (being like the Prince of Peace), the persecuted will inherit the kingdom and receive a great reward. At first, it might seem counterintuitive to say that the persecuted or the mourners or the meek are blessed. But this ignores why exactly they are in such a condition; namely, because of their devotion to the Lord and their living out of the Lord's way of being and behaving. To some extent, one could say that what one gives will be what one gets—the merciful will obtain mercy, the righteous will obtain justice, and so on. But this is because there is a God who makes sure that the moral arc of the world not only satisfies the need for justice and fairness but, in fact, tends toward mercy and love. Notice as well that some of these Beatitudes are about what one does, some are about what happens to a disciple, and some are about what they are or ought to be—for instance, pure in heart or meek. In other words, they are comprehensive in scope. The whole of the disciple's life stands under the grace and blessing of God.

1. What seems strange about these Beatitudes? How do they push us to expand what we mean when we say that God has blessed us?

2. Is Jesus saying these outcomes will happen only in heaven, or is his vision of the final future when Christ returns and the kingdom comes in full on earth, as it is in heaven?

THREE

Antithetical Behavior

Matthew 5:21–48 *"You have heard that it was said to the people long ago, 'You shall not murder, and anyone who murders will be subject to judgment.' ²²But I tell you that anyone who is angry with a brother or sister will be subject to judgment. Again, anyone who says to a brother or sister, 'Raca,' is answerable to the court. And anyone who says, 'You fool!' will be in danger of the fire of hell.*

²³"Therefore, if you are offering your gift at the altar and there remember that your brother or sister has something against you, ²⁴leave your gift there in front of the altar. First go and be reconciled to them; then come and offer your gift.

²⁵"Settle matters quickly with your adversary who is taking you to court. Do it while you are still together on the way, or your adversary may hand you over to the judge, and the judge may hand you over to the officer, and you may be thrown into prison. ²⁶Truly I tell you, you will not get out until you have paid the last penny.

²⁷"You have heard that it was said, 'You shall not commit adultery.' ²⁸But I tell you that anyone who looks at a woman lustfully has already committed adultery with her in his heart. ²⁹If your right eye causes you to stumble, gouge it out and throw it away. It is better for you to lose one part of your body than for your whole body to be thrown into hell. ³⁰And if your right hand causes you to stumble, cut it off and throw it away. It is better for you to lose one part of your body than for your whole body to go into hell.

³¹"It has been said, 'Anyone who divorces his wife must give her a certificate of divorce.' ³²But I tell you that anyone who divorces his wife, except for sexual immorality, makes her the victim of adultery, and anyone who marries a divorced woman commits adultery.

³³"Again, you have heard that it was said to the people long ago, 'Do not break your oath, but fulfill to the Lord the vows you have made.' ³⁴But I tell you, do not swear an oath at all: either by heaven, for it is God's throne; ³⁵or by the earth, for it is his footstool; or by Jerusalem, for it is the city of the Great King. ³⁶And do not swear by your head, for you cannot make even one hair white or black. ³⁷All you need to say is simply 'Yes' or 'No'; anything beyond this comes from the evil one.

³⁸"You have heard that it was said, 'Eye for eye, and tooth for tooth.' ³⁹But I tell you, do not resist an evil person. If anyone slaps you on the right cheek, turn to them the other cheek also. ⁴⁰And if anyone wants to sue you and take your shirt, hand over your coat as well. ⁴¹If anyone forces you to go one mile, go with them two miles. ⁴²Give to the one who asks you, and do not turn away from the one who wants to borrow from you.

⁴³"You have heard that it was said, 'Love your neighbor and hate your enemy.' ⁴⁴But I tell you, love your enemies and pray for those who persecute you, ⁴⁵that you may be children of your Father in heaven. He causes his sun to rise on the evil and the good, and sends rain on the righteous and the unrighteous. ⁴⁶If you love those who love you, what reward will you get? Are not even the tax collectors doing that? ⁴⁷And if you greet only your own people, what are you doing more than others? Do not even pagans do that? ⁴⁸Be perfect, therefore, as your heavenly Father is perfect."

Key Observation. The contrasts between old and new signal that Jesus is not simply reaffirming elements of the Mosaic law. There are genuine contrasts between previous demands in the Old Testament, and the new more intense demands of Jesus.

Understanding the Word. There is much to unpack in this challenging section in the Sermon on the Mount. What is assumed throughout is that by God's grace and mercy, disciples do, indeed, have the capacity to behave in more Christlike ways than previous members of the people of God could and did before Jesus came. Jesus deals with the roots of sin as well as the fruit of sin. He deals with anger and lust and hatred and the negative things that drive negative human behavior. Elsewhere Jesus actually says, "For it is from within, from the human heart, that evil intentions come: fornication, theft, murder, adultery, avarice, wickedness, deceit, licentiousness, envy, slander, pride, folly. All these evil things come from within, and they defile a person" (Mark 7:21–23 NRSV). Jesus is not simply interested in critiquing sinful thoughts and intentions, he is also critiquing the fruit of such thoughts: wicked behavior. He understands that without a radical change of a person's heart, a person will simply fall into one or another of these patterns. They must be born again from the inside if their behavior is going to please God and help other human beings.

A word should be said about the so-called exception clauses regarding divorce both here in Matthew 5:32 and 19:9. The word for adultery is *moixeia* in the Greek and we find it in Matthew 5:27. This is not the word used in 5:32 or 19:9 in the exception clauses, and notice that both Mark 10 and 1 Corinthians 7 tell us that Jesus said "no divorce" in contrast to Moses' teaching. The word we do find in 5:32 and 19:9 is *porneia,* from which we get the word pornography. A *porne* in the world of the New Testament was a prostitute, so it is possible that Jesus is allowing divorce in the case of prostitution. The other specific meaning of the word *porneia* however is "incest," when one marries someone who is related by blood. There was a celebrated incestuous marriage that John the Baptizer critiqued and then lost his head for—the marriage of the ruler of Galilee Herod Antipas to his brother's wife, Herodias (their neice). Jesus may have had in mind that situation—his point would be an incestuous marriage is not a proper marriage in God's eyes to begin with, and so it should be dissolved. The third possibility is that Jesus means by *porneia* all sorts of sexual sins, for sometimes the term can have that sense.

This, however, does not make sense in light of the discussion in 19:1–12, where the disciples clearly react as if Jesus is being more demanding than Moses when it comes to divorce, even saying something like "if the rules are that strict, then better not to marry" (v. 10). And again, Jesus' essential teaching is no divorce of those whom God has joined together as Mark 10 makes quite clear. But perhaps we should also note that Jesus is assuming: (1) that he is referring to two persons who are believers and (2) two persons whom God has joined together. Then, as now, many people married or joined themselves together quite apart from God's will, like Herod Antipas and Herodias. The exception clause is surely speaking about those kinds of situations that are inherently sinful and not in accord with the will of God to begin with.

Finally, the last verse of this section was quite important to John Wesley: "Be perfect, therefore, as your heavenly Father is perfect" (Matt. 5:48). The context shows that Matthew is not talking about perfect persons in the usual moral sense we might take that phrase. The previous verses make clear he is referring to being truly loving, just as the heavenly Father is loving. He is not referring to some sort of experience that perfects a person morally, although it is true that when God pours his love into the human heart it casts out all fear and hate, and cleanses that heart (see Romans 5:5; 1 John 4.8). One's experiences cannot be commanded, but one's behavior can, and so this key verse means "love as the Father loves"—self-sacrificially, continually, wholeheartedly. This is how one fulfills the Law.

1. Why do you think Jesus places so much emphasis on heart purity and heart piety? Isn't most of Matthew 5 about behavior (including the prohibition of divorce for those whom God joined together)?

2. What does it mean to be perfect as the heavenly Father is perfect?

FOUR

The Lord's Prayer

Matthew 6:5–15 *"And when you pray, do not be like the hypocrites, for they love to pray standing in the synagogues and on the street corners to be seen by others. Truly I tell you, they have received their reward in full. ⁶But when you pray, go into your room, close the door and pray to your Father, who is unseen. Then your Father, who sees what is done in secret, will reward you. ⁷And when you pray, do not keep on babbling like pagans, for they think they will be heard because of their many words. ⁸Do not be like them, for your Father knows what you need before you ask him.*

⁹"This, then, is how you should pray: 'Our Father in heaven, hallowed be your name, ¹⁰your kingdom come, your will be done, on earth as it is in heaven. ¹¹Give us today our daily bread. ¹²And forgive us our debts, as we also have forgiven our debtors. ¹³And lead us not into temptation, but deliver us from the evil one.'

¹⁴"For if you forgive other people when they sin against you, your heavenly Father will also forgive you. ¹⁵But if you do not forgive others their sins, your Father will not forgive your sins."

Key Observation. The Lord's Prayer should really be called the disciples' prayer. The prayer is not intended to teach us everything we ought to pray for, but rather the kinds of things we should pray for and about.

Understanding the Word. Matthew's version of the Lord's Prayer should be compared to Luke's less familiar Lukan form in Luke 11:2–4. When one makes such a comparison, it becomes clear that Matthew's form of the prayer has been adapted for community use when the community prays together ("our Father" rather than just "Father"), and Matthew's ends with a doxology of sorts ("for thine is the kingdom . . ."), which reflects it being used in early Christian worship (Matt. 6:13 KJV). Many modern translations do not include the doxology because the earliest copies of Matthew do not include it. It is used traditionally in worship because it clearly reflects how it was used in the church from the earliest centuries of the Christ-following movement. Many scholars have pointed out that this exemplary prayer shows that one should start prayer with adoration ("hallowed be your name"), before making petitions or requests. Further, there is a stress on our praying that God's will, not ours, be done, that God's kingdom, not our success or victory, be accomplished. This is not a prayer for narcissists who think God exists to fulfill our wildest dreams. Indeed, when one is praying for God's kingdom to come, one is praying for the end of the world, for the return of Christ, when the kingdoms of this world will fully become the kingdom of our God and of his Christ. But what the prayer also clearly implies is that right now, God's will is not fully being done on earth, nor has his saving reign fully come on earth yet. You don't petition God for things you already have on earth.

There has been considerable confusion over the next petitions—"lead us not into temptation, but deliver us from evil," as the King James translation has it. In fact, God doesn't lead anyone into temptation, nor can God himself be tempted (see James 1:13). The problem lies with the Greek word *peirasmos*, which can mean either "test" in a good sense, or "tempt" in a bad sense. Since God tempts no one, and does not lead people into the snares of temptation, the better translation would be, "do not put us to the test," followed by, "but rather deliver us from the evil one," who indeed is the tempter. A test, by definition, is meant to strengthen one's character and can come from God, but a temptation comes from the Evil One, and is meant to destroy one's character. Our good and loving God is not in the business of doing the latter.

In the Sermon on the Mount, Jesus teaches us explicitly to seek first the kingdom of God and "all these things will be given to you" (6:33). "All these things" in the context of Matthew 5–6 refers to food, clothing, and shelter. It doesn't refer to the materialistic desires of Americans. Instead, Jesus urges us to pray, "give us today our daily bread" (6:11) or, perhaps, "give us today the bread for tomorrow." If it is the latter, then the point is that the disciple needs the bread now for the next morning in order to not go hungry before the day's work must be done. It reveals the possibility that the disciple may have to at times live from hand to mouth. This is a prayer that encourages us to pray for the necessities of life, and for the total fulfillment of God's plan for humankind on earth. It does not encourage us to pray as if God were a heavenly Santa Claus whose aim is to shower us with whatever gifts we might desire. Finally, our prayers should involve adoration, thanksgiving, petitions about God's will for all of us, and, finally, petitions for and about ourselves. Sadly, we mostly seem to pray "me, me, me" prayers when we should be praying "God, others, and lastly ourselves" prayers.

1. What elements in the Lord's Prayer challenge you the most? Why?

2. What is the difference between a temptation and a test?

FIVE

Do Not Judge, Lest You Be Judged

Matthew 7:1–5 *"Do not judge, or you too will be judged. ²For in the same way you judge others, you will be judged, and with the measure you use, it will be measured to you.*

³"Why do you look at the speck of sawdust in your brother's eye and pay no attention to the plank in your own eye? ⁴How can you say to your brother, 'Let me take the speck out of your eye,' when all the time there is a plank in your own eye? ⁵You hypocrite, first take the plank out of your own eye, and then you will see clearly to remove the speck from your brother's eye."

Key Observation. This famous saying of Jesus is about being self-aware and focusing on dealing with one's own sins and flaws first and foremost. Jesus condemns hypocrisy. He is not forbidding warning others of their sins.

Understanding the Word. Without question, this is one of the most misquoted and misused passages in the whole Sermon on the Mount. Usually, people only recite the opening phrase, conveniently leaving out the "or you too will be judged." The first thing to talk about is what Jesus is actually critiquing here—hypocrisy and exemption from self-criticism. The Greek word *hupocrites,* from which we get hypocrite, literally refers to a play actor, someone playing a part that is not who they actually are. It came to refer to a person who appears or pretends to be one sort of person, but is in fact another—a wolf in sheep's clothing, for example. Here the critique has more to do with the sort of person who does not critically examine himself or herself and work on his or her own flaws, but is rather always criticizing others. Notice that the last line of this teaching says, "first . . . and then . . ." (v. 5). In other words, it's not wrong to criticize the behavior of others, but one ought to first concentrate on getting one's own house in order.

Another element of this teaching is that Jesus contrasts something big obstructing the sight and judgment of the beholder, from some small impediment in the eye of the person who is being critiqued by the first person. Notice as well the reference to "brother" in this teaching. This is not meant to deal with criticism of nonbelievers. This is an in-house matter. Christians do need to hold each other accountable in regard to behavior, and so this is not about Christians casting stones at a lost and sinful world.

The final element of note in this saying is Jesus' warning that a person will be judged in the same manner that they use to judge others. Presumably, this means if you are highly critical of other believers you can expect some searching criticism of yourself when you face the judgment seat of Christ. And yes, the New Testament does teach us that Christ will review and hold us accountable for our deeds. Second Corinthians 5:10 puts it this way: "For we must all appear before the judgment seat of Christ, so that each may receive what is due us for the things done while in the body, whether good or bad." Lest this sound too stern, we can add, fortunately, our judge is also the One who died for and atoned for all our sins—but there will still be an accounting when Christ returns. Think of it this way: when you finally meet the Lord, the only thing you really will want to hear about your behavior is, "well done good and faithful servant, inherit the kingdom" (see Matthew 25:21, 23). We should live to please the Lord always, and hope one day to hear him say that very thing.

1. What sort of judging or critical examination is encouraged in this teaching, and what sort criticized?

2. What does it mean in biblical terms to be a hypocrite?

WEEK TWO

GATHERING DISCUSSION OUTLINE

A. Open session in prayer. Ask that God would astonish us anew with fresh insight from his Word and transform us into the disciples that Jesus desires us to become.

B. View video for this week's readings.

C. What were key insights or takeaways that you gained from your reading during the week and from watching the video commentary? In particular, how did these help you to grow in your faith and understanding of Scripture? What parts of the Bible lesson or study raised questions for you?

D. Discuss questions selected from the daily readings.

    1. **KEY OBSERVATION:** The Sermon on the Mount is a collection of Jesus' core teachings on how his followers should live.

    DISCUSSION QUESTION: Does the Sermon on the Mount simply make radical demands on disciples, or does it provide clues as to how one can live into these commands with God's help?

    2. **KEY OBSERVATION:** The Beatitudes are, in fact, not primarily about our human attitudes, rather they are about the various ways God will bless his people who are poor in spirit, mourning, meek, hungering for a more righteous world, merciful, pure in heart, peacemakers, persecuted, and insulted. In short, God will bless those who behave in Christlike ways.

    DISCUSSION QUESTION: What seems strange about these Beatitudes? How do they push us to expand what we mean when we say that God blessed us?

3. **KEY OBSERVATION:** The contrasts between old and new signal that Jesus is not simply reaffirming elements of the Mosaic law. There are genuine contrasts between previous demands in the Old Testament, and the new more intense demands of Jesus.

    DISCUSSION QUESTION: What does it mean to be perfect as the heavenly Father is perfect?

4. **KEY OBSERVATION:** The Lord's Prayer should really be called the disciples' prayer. The prayer is not intended to teach us everything we ought to pray for, but rather the kinds of things we should pray for and about.

    DISCUSSION QUESTION: What elements in the Lord's Prayer challenge you the most? Why?

5. **KEY OBSERVATION:** This famous saying of Jesus is about being self-aware and focusing on dealing with one's own sins and flaws first and foremost. Jesus condemns hypocrisy. He is not forbidding warning others of their sins.

    DISCUSSION QUESTION: What sort of judging or critical examination is encouraged in this teaching, and what sort criticized?

E. As the study concludes, consider specific ways that this week's Bible lesson invites us to grow and calls us to change. How do this week's scriptures call us to think differently? How do they challenge us to change in order to align ourselves with God's work in the world? What specific actions should we take to apply the insights of the lesson into our daily lives? What kind of person does our Bible lesson call us to become?

F. Close session with prayer. Emphasize God's ongoing work of transformation in our lives in preparation for loving mission and service in the world. Pray for missing class members as well as for persons whom we need to invite to join our study.

WEEK THREE

Matthew 8–9

The Miracles in Matthew

ONE

What Are the Mighty Works of the Kingdom?

Matthew 8:1 *When Jesus came down from the mountainside, large crowds followed him.*

Key Observation. Jesus' miracles are visible signs that God's saving reign (otherwise known as the kingdom) was truly breaking into history in the ministry of Jesus.

Understanding the Word. Matthew has arranged his Gospel such that large blocks of teaching like Matthew 5–7 alternate with accounts of Jesus and the disciples' activities. Matthew 8–9 is the first large block of Jesus' miracle stories. If we ask why the crowds kept following Jesus around, it was not primarily because of his teaching, but rather because so many people needed healing in an age before modern medicine. Matthew presents Jesus as one who proclaims the kingdom in word (5–7) and deed (8–9).

What are we to say about miracles? They are, by definition, things only God and his power can accomplish. There is a difference between the ordinary providence of God, working mundane events together for good, and a miracle. And it's important to distinguish miracles from human attempts at magic. Magic is a human attempt to get hold of some remarkable or divine power and make something happen. It's a bottom-up operation. Miracles are top-down things that are in the hands of God.

Humans cannot make God an offer he can't refuse. It is true, however, that God responds to some human activities with healing and help, for example, genuine prayer and faith. Lack of faith can impede a healing or miracle from happening, but there are plenty of examples in the Gospels, including in Matthew 8–9, where Jesus heals without faith being a prerequisite. The Gadarene demoniacs story is a good example (see Matthew 8:28–34).

And lastly, there is a mystery to all this. Why are some healed and others not? There is not always a one-to-one correlation between genuine faith and healing. Remember the famous story of Paul's earnest request to have God remove his thorn in the flesh (the Greek literally says "a stake in the flesh"). God answered that request with a no, because "My grace is sufficient for you, for my power is made perfect in weakness" (2 Cor. 12:7–10, specifically v. 9).

There are different kinds of miracles—exorcisms, physical healings from things like leprosy, nature miracles (calming of storm, water into wine, fig tree shriveled, walking on water), and the raising of the dead (the widow of Nain's son, the synagogue ruler's daughter). Jesus can perform all of these sorts of miracles, and he does so by the Spirit of God. In fact, he even says at one point that he casts out demons by the Spirit of God (see Matthew 12:28), which fully and richly dwelled in and on Jesus since his baptism. In other words, if we are wondering how the disciples could perform the same mighty works as Jesus, it is because it is the work of the Spirit through Jesus and then through his disciples. The miracles in themselves do not prove Jesus' divinity, for he chose to do them by the power of the Spirit. He operated during his earthly ministry by the power of the Word and the power of the Spirit, just as his disciples can do; the difference being Jesus did not have to deal with the hindrances of sin. Jesus was fully human like us, yet without sin, and at the same time fully divine. Jesus did not draw on his divine capacities (omniscience, omnipotence, and omnipresence) while on this earth so that he could indeed be a model that we, by God's power, can emulate and approximate in terms of trust in God, behavior, and ministry. We are called to do Christlike things; indeed, Jesus even says we will do greater mighty works than he has done (John 14:12–14).

The reason Jesus didn't make miracles his main focus is that propping up this fallen flesh is not God's ultimate aim, because this life is not all there is. There is also the life to come, everlasting life, and more to the point, there is the resurrection of believers yet to come, when we will be fully conformed to Christ's image and have a body immune to disease, decay, death, suffering, sin, and sorrow. Even when Jesus raised the synagogue ruler's daughter (see Matthew 9:18–26), she went on to die again because she was brought back to this life in a mortal body. Temporary miracles are not permanent solutions to our fallen condition. This is why the message of salvation and eternal life was Jesus' main priority, and not the temporary healing of all-too-mortal persons.

1. What counts as a miracle from the biblical perspective, and how should we view them? Will they solve all our problems?

2. Why did Jesus prioritize preaching and teaching over miracle working?

TWO

The Centurion's Servant

Matthew 8:5–13 *When Jesus had entered Capernaum, a centurion came to him, asking for help.*

⁶"Lord," he said, "my servant lies at home paralyzed, suffering terribly."

⁷Jesus said to him, "Shall I come and heal him?"

⁸The centurion replied, "Lord, I do not deserve to have you come under my roof. But just say the word, and my servant will be healed. ⁹For I myself am a man under authority, with soldiers under me. I tell this one, 'Go,' and he goes; and that one, 'Come,' and he comes. I say to my servant, 'Do this,' and he does it."

¹⁰When Jesus heard this, he was amazed and said to those following him, "Truly I tell you, I have not found anyone in Israel with such great faith. ¹¹I say to you that many will come from the east and the west, and will take their places at the feast with Abraham, Isaac and Jacob in the kingdom of heaven. ¹²But the subjects of the kingdom will be thrown outside, into the darkness, where there will be weeping and gnashing of teeth."

¹³Then Jesus said to the centurion, "Go! Let it be done just as you believed it would." And his servant was healed at that moment.

Key Observation. Jesus remarks about the little faith of the disciples at various points and the great faith of outsiders like the centurion.

Understanding the Word. Faith is a living thing. It can grow or shrink, or be entirely absent. It can be strong or weak, and in Matthew's Gospel Jesus quite regularly accosts the disciples by saying "you of little faith" (6:30; 8:26; 14:31; 16:8). The centurion is portrayed as a person who believes Jesus can heal people and that Jesus doesn't have to be present to do so. Jesus can just say the word and the servant can be healed at a distance. This story is meant to make clear just how great Jesus' empowerment by the Spirit was, but it is also a story about trusting Jesus to do something, even when one doesn't see the results immediately or directly. The story ends by telling us that the very moment Jesus said, "Go! Let it be done just as you believed it would," it happened.

Sometimes it does take great faith and trust in God to have a great outcome. This is not because the faith itself does the healing or raising the dead or exorcism. It is because the Healer responds to positive trust in him and his abilities. Let me be clear—the faith that is referred to here is not merely faith that miracles can happen. This is quite specifically faith in God or Jesus that he can accomplish great things. The centurion trusts that Jesus can accomplish things. The centurion could have had ever so much belief in miracles, but if he did not have belief in the Miracle Worker, nothing would have transpired. Nothing. This story is not about faith in faith, or even faith that miracles can occasionally happen. It is about faith in Jesus the Miracle Worker.

One other element in this story requires comment. Jesus suggests that outsiders can become insiders and vice versa when the kingdom finally comes fully on earth. It's all about who has faith in Jesus, and who does not. But these sayings also make clear that Jesus does not believe that, even among God's people, certain ones were predestined from before the foundation of creation to be saved and others lost. No, like most early Jews, Jesus believes that a person can gain faith and lose faith in God, and one's standing in the final kingdom depends on perseverance in trust and belief in Jesus the Miracle Worker.

1. Why is the phrase "miracle-working faith" not quite correct?

2. What does it tell you about Jesus that he will respond to trust in him whether it is by a disciple or an outsider?

THREE
Let the Dead Bury the Dead

Matthew 8:18–22 *When Jesus saw the crowd around him, he gave orders to cross to the other side of the lake. *19Then a teacher of the law came to him and said, "Teacher, I will follow you wherever you go."*

20Jesus replied, "Foxes have dens and birds have nests, but the Son of Man has no place to lay his head."

21Another disciple said to him, "Lord, first let me go and bury my father."

22But Jesus told him, "Follow me, and let the dead bury their own dead."

Key Observation. The cost of discipleship is high, and even family priorities have to give way in the face of Jesus' call that we be his disciples first and before all other priorities in life.

Understanding the Word. Jesus is approached by a Torah scholar (not an ordinary lawyer), and told that the expert in Mosaic law is prepared to follow Jesus wherever he may go. Jesus warns that this may mean being homeless, without food, and the like. It is possible that the use of the term "fox" here alludes to Herod Antipas, because Jesus elsewhere calls him a fox (Luke 13:32). Herod had a nice palace, but Jesus, through rejection by various authority figures and even by his hometown folks, had no permanent home. Jesus suggests the Torah scholar will have to learn how to live on the road, and face rejection rather than normal ancient Near Eastern hospitality.

The second saying in this passage is frankly scandalous. The highest family duty one had to one's parents who have died was to bury them. Jesus is indicating that even those normal, urgent family duties are not more important than following him. Jesus even says, "Let the spiritually dead bury their own [the physically] dead" (Matt. 8:22 NLT). In essence, if you want everlasting life, you'd better hurry up and follow me. It is interesting that the request to bury a father comes from someone who is already a disciple.

One of the recurrent features of these Gospel narratives is that Jesus is not just shocking the outsiders with his teaching, he is consistently shocking the insiders (the disciples) with his extreme demands. This shouldn't have been a repeated occurrence if the disciples had really understood what "take up their cross and follow me" meant (cf. Matthew 16:24). When Jesus makes the call to discipleship using that metaphor, he is, in essence, saying, "You must, in principle, give up everything to follow me. You must see yourself like a condemned man on the way to execution who has lost his freedom of choice and must only do what the Master requires of him. If anything else happens, count it all joy and a bonus, not some right you have to life, liberty, and the pursuit of happiness." For Jesus, the primary family is the family of faith, and sometimes this means that to be Jesus' disciple, one has to leave family and family obligations behind. This is not always the case, but the real disciple of Christ lays it all on the altar and presents himself as a living sacrifice. He is not his own; he has been bought with a price (see 1 Corinthians 6:19–20). Jesus did not come to meet our expectations about family and the good life. He came to call us into his kingdom. As Dietrich Bonhoeffer once said, "When Christ calls a man, he bids him come and die—to self, to selfish priorities, to anything that might get in the way of being a true disciple following Christ and his example."

1. Why do you think Jesus made the cost of discipleship so high? How does Jesus' high bar challenge your understanding of following him?

2. Why do you think so many who encountered Jesus found him more of a threat to normal life than a blessing? More of a threat to one's own pursuit of the good life?

FOUR

Calling an IRS Agent

Matthew 9:9–13 *As Jesus went on from there, he saw a man named Matthew sitting at the tax collector's booth. "Follow me," he told him, and Matthew got up and followed him.*

10While Jesus was having dinner at Matthew's house, many tax collectors and sinners came and ate with him and his disciples. 11When the Pharisees saw this, they asked his disciples, "Why does your teacher eat with tax collectors and sinners?"

12On hearing this, Jesus said, "It is not the healthy who need a doctor, but the sick. 13But go and learn what this means: 'I desire mercy, not sacrifice.' For I have not come to call the righteous, but sinners."

Key Observation. Jesus made a special effort to call sinners and other outsiders into his family, not merely the pious and the Law observant. He was even prepared to banquet with the bad, and says he was especially sent to call the sinners, not the righteous.

Understanding the Word. Here we have yet another example of Jesus' surprising behavior, in this case banqueting with notorious sinners and even with the tax collectors. Indeed, this is a story about calling a tax collector to be one of his twelve disciples! To understand just how shocking this is, one needs to remember that the tax collectors worked for the enemy, Rome, and its client kings like Herod Antipas. Fishermen despised these tax collectors not least because they always took too much in taxes. Graft was rampant because the tax collectors were told by the authorities something like: "I expect you to collect this much for me and whatever else you collect on top of that, you may keep." This was a recipe for disaster and corruption. So now imagine a bunch of disciples that has four fishermen, two tax collectors, and one or two zealots. Talk about a motley crew!

While this story gives the impression that Matthew just up and left his tax collector's desk all of sudden, in fact, if we read all four Gospels carefully, it seems clear that Jesus' calling of disciples took place after they had heard some of his teaching and seen some of his miracles. This is likely the case with Matthew as well. Jesus had no issues with dining at Matthew's house, even when the guest list included a lot more tax collectors and sinners. Jesus was not concerned about being made unclean by contact with such persons; indeed, he went to them to cleanse, heal, and save them. And we get a strong sense of his priorities when it comes to the Law as well. In his view, the heart of Torah is mercy, or to use another familiar term, loving-kindness. This is the core character of God, and it is also at the core of Jesus' character. Jesus wanted the least, the last, and the lost to become the most, the first, and the found. Indeed, Jesus believed there would be some very surprising participants in the kingdom that was coming.

As for the question of the Pharisees as to why Jesus banqueted with the bad, of course we would answer it is because he came to save them. But from the Pharisees' viewpoint, a holy person would not do something like that, not primarily due to ritual purity concerns, but due to moral purity concerns: one would get a reputation of hanging out with the wrong crowd. Many years ago when I was a pastor, I went and visited a troubled parishioner at a bar. He wanted a neutral site that he was comfortable with, and I had no problem with that. However, the gossip mill cranked up, and I had people ask me why in the world I was in a bar. I was even told that it was not appropriate for ministers and reflected badly on their church. I explained what I was doing, and most of the objections fell by the wayside, but they were telling. Some were more concerned with their church's reputation than with saving sinners. I was more concerned with the latter, and sometimes one has to be prepared to be thought poorly of to actually do the work Jesus calls us to do.

1. Think about Matthew joining the band of disciples. What challenges appear when outsiders become insiders?

2. Why is mercy the essence of the gospel and Jesus' top priority?

FIVE

Jairus and the Jewess

Matthew 9:18–26 *While he was saying this, a synagogue leader came and knelt before him and said, "My daughter has just died. But come and put your hand on her, and she will live." ¹⁹Jesus got up and went with him, and so did his disciples.*

²⁰Just then a woman who had been subject to bleeding for twelve years came up behind him and touched the edge of his cloak. ²¹She said to herself, "If I only touch his cloak, I will be healed."

²²Jesus turned and saw her. "Take heart, daughter," he said, "your faith has healed you." And the woman was healed at that moment.

²³When Jesus entered the synagogue leader's house and saw the noisy crowd and people playing pipes, ²⁴he said, "Go away. The girl is not dead but asleep." But they laughed at him. ²⁵After the crowd had been put outside, he went in and took the girl by the hand, and she got up. ²⁶News of this spread through all that region.

Key Observation. Jesus is prepared to help and heal, even when it interrupts what he is setting out to do, and even when the situation seems hopeless.

Understanding the Word. Matthew tells a greatly abbreviated version of the healing stories in Mark 5:21–43. Matthew cuts out many details (such as the name of the synagogue leader) to put the focus solely on Jesus as the One who is willing and able to heal those who are in need. Let's explore this narrative.

The action begins with a synagogue leader (Jairus) coming to Jesus. He believes Jesus can raise the dead. He falls on his knees and makes his appeal for his dead daughter, and Jesus and the disciples go at once with him.

Suddenly, a woman who has suffered with a blood flow, presumably menstrual in nature, for twelve years appears and tells herself that she can be healed if she just touches the fringes of the robe of the Miracle Worker. The fringes were regular Jewish features of men's robes, indicating they were keeping the Mosaic law. It was often believed in that age that contact with a holy man, even with his garments, could produce healing. One should compare the famous story of Paul and the healing hankies (see Acts 19:11–12). And, indeed, the woman is suddenly cured after suffering for twelve years, but not before Jesus tells her to take heart and that she would be healed through her faith in him. Jesus does not want the woman to have faith in holy garments. So he says to her, "your faith has healed you" (i.e., not the garment). The verb actually used here is the verb "saved," meaning "healed," "helped," "rescued," as it regularly does in the Old Testament.

Matthew expands on Mark's version; namely, that there were professional mourners already present and playing sad music at the ruler's house. It is probably they who laugh when Jesus says she wasn't dead but sleeping. Jesus is annoyed by phony. More important, Jesus believes that even death is not permanent in his hands. Yes, the girl was truly dead, but in the hands of Jesus the Raiser of the Dead and the Resurrection and the Life, death is no more permanent than sleep. It is something one can come back from refreshed and renewed. God's yes to life is louder than death's no. Jesus is not suggesting that one snoozes in the afterlife; he is not an advocate of the idea called soul sleep. He is simply drawing an analogy between sleep and death. When one believes in resurrection, death is no longer seen as permanent (see the same sort of language from Paul in 1 Thessalonians 4).

The story ends with a report of how news of this miracle spread around the region.

1. What impression does this story give you about Jesus as a healer? Does he perform miracles in order to persuade people to believe in him, or are they mainly just acts of compassion?

2. How does Jesus act to correct the bleeding woman's magic-tainted faith and elevate it to a true understanding of how and why she was healed?

WEEK THREE

GATHERING DISCUSSION OUTLINE

A. Open session in prayer. Ask that God would astonish us anew with fresh insight from his Word and transform us into the disciples that Jesus desires us to become.

B. View video for this week's readings.

C. What were key insights or takeaways that you gained from your reading during the week and from watching the video commentary? In particular, how did these help you to grow in your faith and understanding of Scripture? What parts of the Bible lesson or study raised questions for you?

D. Discuss questions selected from the daily readings.

   1. **KEY OBSERVATION:** Jesus' miracles are visible signs that God's saving reign (otherwise known as the kingdom) was truly breaking into history in the ministry of Jesus.

   DISCUSSION QUESTION: What counts as a miracle from the biblical perspective, and how should we view them? Will they solve all our problems?

   2. **KEY OBSERVATION:** Jesus remarks about the little faith of the disciples at various points and the great faith of outsiders like the centurion.

   DISCUSSION QUESTION: What does it tell you about Jesus that he will respond to trust in him whether it is by a disciple or an outsider?

3. **KEY OBSERVATION:** The cost of discipleship is high, and even family priorities have to give way in the face of Jesus' call that we be his disciples first and before all other priorities in life.

    DISCUSSION QUESTION: Why do you think Jesus made the cost of discipleship so high? How does Jesus' high bar challenge your understanding of following him?

4. **KEY OBSERVATION:** Jesus made a special effort to call sinners and other outsiders into his family, not merely the pious and the Law observant. He was even prepared to banquet with the bad, and says he was especially sent to call the sinners, not the righteous.

    DISCUSSION QUESTION: Think about Matthew joining the band of disciples. What challenges appear when outsiders become insiders?

5. **KEY OBSERVATION:** Jesus is prepared to help and heal, even when it interrupts what he is setting out to do, and even when the situation seems hopeless.

    DISCUSSION QUESTION: How does Jesus act to correct the bleeding woman's magic-tainted faith and elevate it to a true understanding of how and why she was healed?

E. As the study concludes, consider specific ways that this week's Bible lesson invites us to grow and calls us to change. How do this week's scriptures call us to think differently? How do they challenge us to change in order to align ourselves with God's work in the world? What specific actions should we take to apply the insights of the lesson into our daily lives? What kind of person does our Bible lesson call us to become?

F. Close session with prayer. Emphasize God's ongoing work of transformation in our lives in preparation for loving mission and service in the world. Pray for missing class members as well as for persons whom we need to invite to join our study.

WEEK FOUR

Matthew 11–12

The Many Images of Jesus

ONE

Jesus the Revealer and Jesus the Revelation

Matthew 11:25–27 *At that time Jesus said, "I praise you, Father, Lord of heaven and earth, because you have hidden these things from the wise and learned, and revealed them to little children. *[26]*Yes, Father, for this is what you were pleased to do.*

[27]"All things have been committed to me by my Father. No one knows the Son except the Father, and no one knows the Father except the Son and those to whom the Son chooses to reveal him."*

Key Observation. The key to understanding Jesus is recognizing his unique relationship with his Father.

Understanding the Word. This text speaks to us about Jesus being both a revealer and the revelation of God. The presupposition behind these verses is that, unless God reveals himself, fallen human beings will not understand him. So he chooses to reveal himself exclusively through his Son. In fact, Jesus says that no one knows the Father but him (an astounding claim), and that only the Father thus far truly knows the Son. Further, Jesus stresses that all things have been committed to him by the Father. In this case, "all things" has to do with the revelation of the coming final kingdom of God, of God's coming final saving activity, and of the *bringing* (not merely announcing) of that saving activity. Jesus' life, death, and resurrection are central to this mission.

An assumption in this text is that the hearts of God's people have grown hard. They have not been listening to God's messengers. Thus, God has to send his own Son to reveal and implement God's saving truth. The people dwell in darkness, and only a direct revelation from God, in this case in the person of his Son, can help them. But why would God hide these things from the wise and reveal them to children or those lacking experience?

Perhaps we are meant to think that the worldly wise have ceased to be open to anything new. We see this sort of cynical wisdom in the book of Ecclesiastes, where there is the mantra—"there is nothing new under the sun" (1:9). But perhaps this is also what happens when a person gets too familiar with the ways of the fallen world. We forget that God can do new things in the lives of people. Children at least are mostly without guile, without cynicism. There is an openness in children; they are ready to receive a new revelation from God. Their lack of experience in this world is a plus in that case.

1. What does it tell you about Jesus that he claims exclusive access to the Father?

2. What can we learn from children to help us have eyes and ears capable of receiving truth from God?

TWO

Jesus as the Wisdom of God with a New Yoke

Matthew 11:28–30 *"Come to me, all you who are weary and burdened, and I will give you rest. [29] Take my yoke upon you and learn from me, for I am gentle and humble in heart, and you will find rest for your souls. [30] For my yoke is easy and my burden is light."*

Key Observation. Jesus presented himself in many ways during his ministry that did not always conform to traditional expectations of what the Messiah would be like. Some of these, like the Son of Man, were based in a specific prophecy in Daniel 7, but others were based more generally in early Jewish Wisdom Literature (in this case, Sirach).

Understanding the Word. Understanding Matthew's presentation of Jesus requires understanding earlier Jewish literature both in the Old Testament and in intertestamental Jewish literature not found in the Old Testament. Our text for today clearly echoes the Wisdom material in Wisdom of Solomon, and Sirach, two popular earlier Jewish books. For example, in Sirach 6:23–28 (NABRE) we hear this spoken of personified Wisdom:

> Listen, my child, and take my advice;
>> do not refuse my counsel.
> Put your feet into her fetters,
>> and your neck under her yoke.
> Bend your shoulders and carry her
>> and do not be irked at her bonds.
>
> With all your soul draw close to her;
>> and with all your strength keep her ways.
> Inquire and search, seek and find;
>> when you get hold of her, do not let her go.
> Thus at last you will find rest in her,
>> and she will become your joy.

And from Sirach 51:25–27 (NABRE):

> I open my mouth and speak of her:
>> gain wisdom for yourselves at no cost.
>
> Take her yoke upon your neck;
>> that your mind may receive her teaching.
> For she is close to those who seek her,
>> and the one who is in earnest finds her.
>
> See for yourselves! I have labored only a little,
>> but have found much.

A close study of Sirach shows that the author, Jesus ben Sira, is speaking about Wisdom as it is found especially in the Old Testament. The similarities to what Jesus is saying are eye-opening. Jesus is saying that instead of taking on the yoke of Torah, of the Mosaic law, his followers should take on his yoke, which, in something of an oxymoron, is called a light burden or an easy yoke!

He is talking about his own wisdom teaching, which we have already explored in the Sermon on the Mount (Matthew 5–7). But Jesus is not merely identifying his teaching as wise. He is identifying himself as God's wisdom come in the flesh. Earlier in Matthew 11:19, he identifies himself directly as Wisdom saying, "Yet wisdom is vindicated by [his] deeds" (NRSV).

Notice as well that Jesus is not only said to know the mind of God, as is said of Wisdom in Proverbs 8–9, but here in Matthew 11:27 Jesus says that he alone knows and reveals the Father, and that he has a unique and exclusive relationship with the Father as well. Jesus presents himself as being the exclusive mediator and revealer of the nature and character of God the Father.

1. A yoke is an emblem of hard work. What do you think Jesus meant when he said his yoke was easy and his burden light?

2. Jesus puts himself in the position of Wisdom here, offering his yoke, as opposed to the yoke of the Mosaic law. Why do you think he does this?

THREE

Jesus and the Servant Songs

Matthew 12:15–21 *Aware of this, Jesus withdrew from that place. A large crowd followed him, and he healed all who were ill. ¹⁶He warned them not to tell others about him. ¹⁷This was to fulfill what was spoken through the prophet Isaiah:*

¹⁸"Here is my servant whom I have chosen, the one I love, in whom I delight; I will put my Spirit on him, and he will proclaim justice to the nations. ¹⁹He will not quarrel or cry out; no one will hear his voice in the streets. ²⁰A bruised reed he will not break, and a smoldering wick he will not snuff out, till he has brought justice through to victory. ²¹In his name the nations will put their hope."

Key Observation. Another way that Jesus understood his role as Messiah was through the imagery of Isaiah's Suffering Servant (Isaiah 40–55).

Understanding the Word. Another way Jesus presents himself is by drawing on the Servant material from Isaiah. In general, Isaiah 40–55 has been called the Servant Songs. In Matthew 12, Isaiah 42:1–4 is quoted directly as a prophecy that Jesus fulfilled. Jesus fulfills this prophecy through his mighty acts of healing and justice, as well as through his teaching and preaching. On the one hand, because God's Spirit is on him he will proclaim justice to the nations. And on the other hand, he will take up the cause of the oppressed, the downtrodden, those who have been beaten, bruised, harmed, abused, and whose spiritual life is at a low ebb and needs reviving. Jesus is the fulfillment of all sorts of prophecies and promises in the Old Testament, and not just the traditional ones like in 2 Samuel 7:12–14 about a descendant of David coming as a great king. Jesus did not come to meet the expectations of his people; he came to meet their needs and reveal himself in his own way and in his own good time.

1. How can one be both a proclaimer of justice to the nations and a dispenser of mercy to the downtrodden?

2. Why do you think Jesus envisioned himself as the Servant of Isaiah 40–55, knowing that Isaiah 52:13–53:12 indicates the Servant will be despised, rejected, and killed?

FOUR

Jesus and Jonah and One Greater than Solomon

Matthew 12:38–42 *Then some of the Pharisees and teachers of the law said to him, "Teacher, we want to see a sign from you."*

[39]He answered, "A wicked and adulterous generation asks for a sign! But none will be given it except the sign of the prophet Jonah. [40]For as Jonah was three days and three nights in the belly of a huge fish, so the Son of Man will be three days and three nights in the heart of the earth. [41]The men of Nineveh will stand up at the judgment with this generation and condemn it; for they repented at the preaching of Jonah, and now something greater than Jonah is here. [42]The Queen of the South will rise at the judgment with this generation and condemn it; for she came from the ends of the earth to listen to Solomon's wisdom, and now something greater than Solomon is here."

Key Observation. Jesus draws an analogy between himself and Jonah, and also himself and Solomon, which is to say an analogy with a reluctant prophet and a king famous for his wisdom.

Understanding the Word. This passage is interesting on many levels. First of all, notice the adversarial context in which Jesus gives these sayings. The Jewish religious leaders ask Jesus for a sign. In this case, they are referring to a validating sign, something that could prove Jesus is who he says he is. All along Jesus has been performing miracles, and yet apparently that is not enough for these people. They want direct proof of Jesus' identity. They have forgotten that it is believing that leads to seeing, rather than seeing leading to believing. The authorities would later know that Jesus raised Lazarus from the dead, some of them being present to see the event, and yet this did not move or convert them.

And so Jesus refuses to give a validating proof of his identity. Instead, he speaks about Jonah the reluctant prophet, swallowed by a great fish while he is running away from God, and yet miraculously rescued by God. With hindsight, we know that Jesus is alluding to his coming death and rescue from beyond the grave by means of resurrection, but his audience had not been trained to think of a dying and rising Messiah, much less a crucified one. Jesus' saying would have been enigmatic to this unresponsive audience that he identifies as part of a wicked generation of God's people. That generation will be judged by the repentant Ninevites (Jonah 3) and the Queen of the South, the Queen of Sheba who visited Solomon (1 Kings 10:1–13).

Jesus concludes this teaching by saying that "something greater than Solomon" was present in their midst, and they didn't even realize it. Jesus says "something" rather than "someone." Jesus is referring to the fact that he is the embodiment of God's Wisdom ("something") come in the flesh to reveal God's saving truth to his people.

This reference to Solomon clarifies the meaning of "Son of David" that we see in Matthew's Gospel. The son of David was, of course, Solomon, and in Jesus' day Solomon was thought to possess the wisdom of all sorts of cures, even of exorcisms. So when Jesus is called son of David by needy people like the two blind men (Matthew 20:29), they are referring to their need for healing. Here in a different way Jesus is admitting he is like Solomon, only greater. Solomon had wisdom; but, more profoundly, Jesus was God's Wisdom come in person.

1. What is the sign of Jonah? What does it teach us about Jesus?

2. What did Jesus mean when he said "something greater than Solomon is here"?

FIVE

The Family of Faith

Matthew 12:46–50 *While Jesus was still talking to the crowd, his mother and brothers stood outside, wanting to speak to him.* *⁴⁷Someone told him, "Your mother and brothers are standing outside, wanting to speak to you."*

⁴⁸He replied to him, "Who is my mother, and who are my brothers?" ⁴⁹Pointing to his disciples, he said, "Here are my mother and my brothers. ⁵⁰For whoever does the will of my Father in heaven is my brother and sister and mother."

Key Observation. For Jesus, the primary family is the family of faith, not the physical family.

Understanding the Word. It is instructive to compare Matthew's version of this saying with Mark 3:21, 31–35. Matthew completely omits 3:21, which says that the family came to take Jesus home because they thought he was out of his right mind! Matthew omits this controversial verse, but he makes even more explicit that Jesus is contrasting the family of faith with his physical family by saying that Jesus pointed to his disciples when he said, "Here are my mother and brothers." Mark does not mention the pointing. The family Jesus is forming is based on "whoever does the will of my Father." Ties of kinship take a second place to ties of faith and the doing of God's will. You see something like this as well in the Elijah/Elisha narrative when Elijah calls Elisha away from his family to be a prophet in training with Elijah (1 Kings 19). Jesus, then, is not merely forming a new religious community or movement, he is forming a new family. This family of faith is supposed to take priority over the physical family when it comes to doing God's will. This is why earlier in Matthew 10:34–36 we hear Jesus say:

> "Do not suppose that I have come to bring peace to the earth. I did not come to bring peace, but a sword. For I have come to turn
> "'a man against his father,
> a daughter against her mother,
> a daughter-in-law against her mother-in-law—
> a man's enemies will be the members of his own household.'"

The point of such a difficult saying is that following Jesus and being part of his family of faith comes first in the order of priorities. But what if the whole family is united in the following of Jesus, like for instance the family of Mary, Martha, and Lazarus (see Luke 10:38–42 and John 11)? At the end of the day, Jesus was radical, and he still is today. What usually is called family values today is not exactly what Jesus meant when he talked about who were his mothers and brothers and sisters. In a culture full of broken and dysfunctional physical families, this teaching can be seen as a balm rather than a bane, a blessing rather than a curse. If the church will just be a family for single persons, married persons, parents and children, and they are taught that they are part of a larger, worldwide, nurturing family of faith, they can have healed and healthy relationships in the Lord and with one another.

1. What do you think Jesus' relationship with his family was like, based on this text?

2. How does following Jesus affect your relationships with your own family? How does it support your roles within your family? What are the points of tension?

WEEK FOUR

GATHERING DISCUSSION OUTLINE

A. Open session in prayer. Ask that God would astonish us anew with fresh insight from his Word and transform us into the disciples that Jesus desires us to become.

B. View video for this week's readings.

C. What were key insights or takeaways that you gained from your reading during the week and from watching the video commentary? In particular, how did these help you to grow in your faith and understanding of Scripture? What parts of the Bible lesson or study raised questions for you?

D. Discuss questions selected from the daily readings.

1. **KEY OBSERVATION:** The key to understanding Jesus is recognizing his unique relationship with his Father.

DISCUSSION QUESTION: What can we learn from children to help us have eyes and ears capable of receiving truth from God?

2. **KEY OBSERVATION:** Jesus presented himself in many ways during his ministry that did not always conform to traditional expectations of what the Messiah would be like. Some of these, like the Son of Man, were based in a specific prophecy in Daniel 7, but others were based more generally in early Jewish Wisdom Literature (in this case, Sirach).

DISCUSSION QUESTION: A yoke is an emblem of hard work. What do you think Jesus meant when he said his yoke was easy and his burden light?

3. **KEY OBSERVATION:** Another way that Jesus understood his role as Messiah was through the imagery of Isaiah's Suffering Servant (Isaiah 40–55).

   DISCUSSION QUESTION: How can one be both a proclaimer of justice to the nations and a dispenser of mercy to the downtrodden?

4. **KEY OBSERVATION:** Jesus draws an analogy between himself and Jonah, and also himself and Solomon, which is to say an analogy with a reluctant prophet and a king famous for his wisdom.

   DISCUSSION QUESTION: What did Jesus mean when he said "something greater than Solomon is here"?

5. **KEY OBSERVATION:** For Jesus, the primary family is the family of faith, not the physical family.

   DISCUSSION QUESTION: How does following Jesus affect your relationships with your own family? How does it support your roles within your family? What are the points of tension?

E. As the study concludes, consider specific ways that this week's Bible lesson invites us to grow and calls us to change. How do this week's scriptures call us to think differently? How do they challenge us to change in order to align ourselves with God's work in the world? What specific actions should we take to apply the insights of the lesson into our daily lives? What kind of person does our Bible lesson call us to become?

F. Close session with prayer. Emphasize God's ongoing work of transformation in our lives in preparation for loving mission and service in the world. Pray for missing class members as well as for persons whom we need to invite to join our study.

WEEK FIVE

Matthew 13

The Parables of Jesus

ONE

All Things in Parables

Matthew 13:1–9 *That same day Jesus went out of the house and sat by the lake.* *²Such large crowds gathered around him that he got into a boat and sat in it, while all the people stood on the shore. ³Then he told them many things in parables, saying: "A farmer went out to sow his seed. ⁴As he was scattering the seed, some fell along the path, and the birds came and ate it up. ⁵Some fell on rocky places, where it did not have much soil. It sprang up quickly, because the soil was shallow. ⁶But when the sun came up, the plants were scorched, and they withered because they had no root. ⁷Other seed fell among thorns, which grew up and choked the plants. ⁸Still other seed fell on good soil, where it produced a crop—a hundred, sixty or thirty times what was sown. ⁹Whoever has ears, let them hear."*

Key Observation. Jesus used parables for his public teaching to the crowds.

Understanding the Word. A *parabolos*, or in Hebrew a *mashal*, is a form of metaphorical speech, drawing an analogy between an ordinary aspect of life and an aspect of God's divine saving activity or dominion. There are some forty or so parables in the Gospels, none of which are in John's Gospel, which simply omits them.

Jesus' parables are always about what we call the kingdom or reign of God. In other words they are about God's attempts to establish his kingdom, his saving reign (or rule) on earth as it is in heaven, and, in this case, doing it through the ministry of his Son. Another important aspect of Jesus' kingdom sayings (shared also by Paul in his letters) is that when Jesus is speaking about the kingdom in the present tense, the term has an active, verbal sense; it refers to God's saving activity resulting in God's reign in a human life or group of people. On the other hand, when Jesus or Paul is speaking about the kingdom or dominion in the future tense, they are talking about a place, and so the term has a noun sense. This is when you hear the language of "entering" or "inheriting" or "seeing" (rather than experiencing internally) the kingdom of God. In our day, we are still praying for the full rule of God on earth as it is in heaven, and when that finally happens at Jesus' return, then and then only will the kingdoms of this world become God's kingdom. In the meanwhile, we see the precursors of this when Christ becomes the Lord or King of someone's life and begins to rule over their everyday existence. Then, we become places where the divine saving activity of God is in evidence. So, for instance, Jesus says, "But if it is by the Spirit of God that I cast out demons, then the kingdom of God has come to you" (Matt. 12:28 NRSV).

In some ways, the parable of the sower is the most paradigmatic of all parables because it talks about the relationship between Jesus' ministry and the coming of the kingdom on earth. Jesus understands his ministry as simply sowing the good news of God's saving activity. The key distinction in the parable of the sower is not the sower or the seeds, but the differences in the soils; rocky, shallow, thorny/weedy, and good soil. Jesus says that the seed (a.k.a. the Word of the gospel) should be scattered freely, but the outcomes will vary according to the conditions of the soils.

Parables are not full-blown allegories like, for instance, John Bunyan's *Pilgrim's Progress*. But they clearly have allegorical elements such that some features from within the parable are actually commentary on something outside the parable itself, hence seed as the Word of God. But not every aspect of the parable has an analogy with the kingdom. Sometimes interpreters make the mistake of turning every detail in a parable into a symbol for something else. For example, the early church leader Augustine allegorized the parable of the good Samaritan. He suggested the good Samaritan represented Christ, the man lying on the side of the road represented people dead in trespasses, the oil and wine administered to the man represented the sacraments, the inn represented the church, and so on. This simply was not Jesus' intended message. Samaritans were real people, cousins of the Jews, and the two groups did not get along. So that parable is actually a social commentary on a problem that existed in Jesus' own day. We need to not read any symbols into a parable that are not suggested within the biblical text itself. In the parable of the sower, Jesus adds an interpretation of the parable in Matthew 13:18–23.

Another mistake often made in interpreting these parables is assuming they are true to agricultural life in the ancient world. This is mostly false. Farmers would first clear the land of stones, thorns, and the like, plow it, and then scatter the seed. They would not waste good seed by throwing it on unprepared land. The parables are true to the kingdom, and not entirely true to ancient Jewish life in Jesus' day.

In the end, the parable of the sower tells us that the ministry of Jesus and his disciples thereafter would have many disappointments—many people would reject the good news. But the harvest, the positive outcome, would be so great, that the divine reign would show up in significant ways in many lives that heard the Word of divine redemption through Jesus. It also invites us as readers to ponder what sort of soil is in our hearts.

1. What does the parable of the sower tell us about Jesus' ministry and approach?

2. What type of soil are you? How would you need to change in order to be good soil consistently?

TWO

Why Parables?

Matthew 13:10–17 *The disciples came to him and asked, "Why do you speak to the people in parables?"*

11He replied, "Because the knowledge of the secrets of the kingdom of heaven has been given to you, but not to them. 12Whoever has will be given more, and they will have an abundance. Whoever does not have, even what they have will be taken from them. 13This is why I speak to them in parables: Though seeing, they do not see; though hearing, they do not hear or understand.

14"In them is fulfilled the prophecy of Isaiah: 'You will be ever hearing but never understanding; you will be ever seeing but never perceiving. 15For this people's heart has become calloused; they hardly hear with their ears, and they have closed their eyes. Otherwise they might see with their eyes, hear with their ears, understand with their hearts and turn, and I would heal them.'

¹⁶"But blessed are your eyes because they see, and your ears because they hear. ¹⁷For truly I tell you, many prophets and righteous people longed to see what you see but did not see it, and to hear what you hear but did not hear it."

Key Observation. Jesus spoke in parables to convey to the crowds that their hearts were hard and, unless they repented and turned to him, they would not understand his message.

Understanding the Word. The first key in understanding this difficult passage is to recognize that Jesus is quoting from Isaiah 6:9–13. Isaiah received these words from God as part of his call to ministry. His mission was to make clear to God's people that they were alienated from God due to their hardness. Jesus, who sometimes uses the phrase "this wicked generation" believes his own audience is, in general, in the same state of spiritual danger as the audience of Isaiah's original saying. But there is a glimmer of hope at the end of the quotation; namely, that if God's people will repent of their sins and turn back to God, suddenly God's Word will make sense; it will become clear again and they can be reconciled once more to God. In addition, Jesus affirms that the secrets of the kingdom will be more fully explained to the disciples in their private discussions.

This explanation of Jesus' rationale for speaking in parables rules out the explanation that Jesus was a master storyteller who taught simple truths. To the contrary, parables violate what many assume to be the first rule of communication—be clear and speak in a way that your audience can easily understand. This was not Jesus' approach to the hard of heart. As British New Testament scholar C. H. Dodd once said, parables are meant to tease the mind. Their meaning must be pondered deeply before understanding can come. Sometimes, like the first disciples, one needs additional help to decipher them. Parables are not plain speech; they are indirect and highly metaphorical speech.

1. What does the quote from Isaiah suggest to you about how Jesus viewed the spiritual condition of most of his audience, and why exactly he addressed them in indirect ways?

2. What role does repentance and turning to God play in helping a person understand God's Word?

THREE
The Parable of the Sower Explained

Matthew 13:18–23 *"Listen then to what the parable of the sower means:* [19]*When anyone hears the message about the kingdom and does not understand it, the evil one comes and snatches away what was sown in their heart. This is the seed sown along the path.* [20]*The seed falling on rocky ground refers to someone who hears the word and at once receives it with joy.* [21]*But since they have no root, they last only a short time. When trouble or persecution comes because of the word, they quickly fall away.* [22]*The seed falling among the thorns refers to someone who hears the word, but the worries of this life and the deceitfulness of wealth choke the word, making it unfruitful.* [23]*But the seed falling on good soil refers to someone who hears the word and understands it. This is the one who produces a crop, yielding a hundred, sixty or thirty times what was sown."*

Key Observation. Jesus explains the parable to encourage his disciples, but also to give a warning about obstacles to discipleship.

Understanding the Word. There are many things that can get in the way of hearing and receiving God's Word from Jesus, and not all of them have to do with spiritual hardening of the arteries. Jesus doesn't throw all the seed on the hard path. Sometimes the cares and anxieties of life crowd out hearing, understanding, and believing God's Word. Sometimes the Devil himself intervenes and distracts the listener, or turns him off to the message.

Jesus is sometimes accused of utopian teaching, expecting far too much of his followers who sometimes seem more like the DUH-sciples than proper disciples. But, in fact, the teaching of the parable of the sower is realistic. Jesus is saying that the disciples, when they share God's good news, will find that many times the response will be negative, short-lived, or they will have no response at all. But the end of the parable provides good reason for hope. For those who are good soil, and receive the seed, the fruit that will be borne out of that soil will be a bumper crop, a vast harvest. Those who labor in the Lord ultimately never labor in vain.

The story is told of a small-church British minister who had never had much success, never been offered a bigger church, and never seemed likely to accomplish much more than maintaining the little church he had. However, there was one young man into whom he poured a lot of time and energy. He discipled this young man for many years. It was his one major ray of hope that he was doing good ministry. As it turned out, he was right. The young man was Charles Spurgeon, who went on to have a worldwide ministry touching the lives of many people. The parable in Matthew 13, like this story, should remind us that worldly measures of success, such as stupendous church growth, are not the way God measures success. As Jesus' realistic parable suggests, followers of Jesus should expect considerable failures and difficulties, but the singular successes, those who are really brought to the Lord or properly discipled, will produce the kind of harvest that will seem miraculous. A good harvest in Jesus' day was perhaps ten or twentyfold, but Jesus says that in the kingdom the results can be nothing short of miraculous even if they involve just a single tiny patch of good soil.

1. What obstacles hinder you the most in your following of Jesus—anxieties about life, persecution, or the desire for great wealth?

2. How does the parable of the sower encourage God's people to serve faithfully?

FOUR

The Parables of the Weeds, the Seeds, and the Yeast

Matthew 13:24–43 *Jesus told them another parable: "The kingdom of heaven is like a man who sowed good seed in his field. ²⁵But while everyone was sleeping, his enemy came and sowed weeds among the wheat, and went away. ²⁶When the wheat sprouted and formed heads, then the weeds also appeared.*

²⁷"The owner's servants came to him and said, 'Sir, didn't you sow good seed in your field? Where then did the weeds come from?'

²⁸"'An enemy did this,' he replied.

"The servants asked him, 'Do you want us to go and pull them up?'

²⁹"'No,' he answered, 'because while you are pulling the weeds, you may uproot the wheat with them. ³⁰Let both grow together until the harvest. At that time, I will tell the harvesters: First collect the weeds and tie them in bundles to be burned; then gather the wheat and bring it into my barn.'"

³¹He told them another parable: "The kingdom of heaven is like a mustard seed, which a man took and planted in his field. ³²Though it is the smallest of all seeds, yet when it grows, it is the largest of garden plants and becomes a tree, so that the birds come and perch in its branches."

³³He told them still another parable: "The kingdom of heaven is like yeast that a woman took and mixed into about sixty pounds of flour until it worked all through the dough."

³⁴Jesus spoke all these things to the crowd in parables; he did not say anything to them without using a parable. ³⁵So was fulfilled what was spoken through the prophet: "I will open my mouth in parables, I will utter things hidden since the creation of the world."

³⁶Then he left the crowd and went into the house. His disciples came to him and said, "Explain to us the parable of the weeds in the field."

³⁷He answered, "The one who sowed the good seed is the Son of Man. ³⁸The field is the world, and the good seed stands for the people of the kingdom. The weeds are the people of the evil one, ³⁹and the enemy who sows them is the devil. The harvest is the end of the age, and the harvesters are angels.

⁴⁰"As the weeds are pulled up and burned in the fire, so it will be at the end of the age. ⁴¹The Son of Man will send out his angels, and they will weed out of his kingdom everything that causes sin and all who do evil. ⁴²They will throw them into the blazing furnace, where there will be weeping and gnashing of teeth.⁴³Then the righteous will shine like the sun in the kingdom of their Father. Whoever has ears, let them hear."

Key Observation. Jesus warns that disciples can't fully identify kingdom people until the kingdom fully comes on earth and God separates the wheat from the weeds.

Understanding the Word. All of these parables in Matthew 13 contrast how things appear at the beginning with how things turn out in the end, but in different ways. In one sense the parable of the wheat and weeds is a cautionary tale reminding the disciples not to try and weed people out of the community prematurely. For it is God, in the end, not us, that sorts out the wheat from the weeds. The community of Christ will be wheat and weeds until the Lord returns. We should not presume to be judge, jury, and executioner of someone else's spiritual life and destiny.

The parable of the mustard seed and the yeast provide evidence that Jesus may have originally told parables in pairs, one that spoke more to the males in his audience (planting) and one to the female disciples (yeast put in dough). Both parables contrast tiny beginnings with results that seem out of all proportion to the size of the seed or the yeast. Some scholars have questioned whether anyone would actually plant a mustard seed, which has sometimes been said to be a noxious weed, not something a farmer would plant. This is missing the point that the parable is about small beginnings and outrageously huge outcomes. It is, however, possible that the reference to the birds nesting in the giant mustard bush is a reference to outsiders, perhaps even Gentiles becoming part of the kingdom of God unexpectedly.

Two other things one should gather from these particular parables. Jesus believes there is a devil working woe in this world, including in the midst of God's people and even Jesus' disciples. Furthermore, Jesus believes in final judgment; he believes some people will receive a positive and some people a negative afterlife and, thus, what we believe and how we behave affects, indeed to some degree determines, our eternal destiny. Shining like the sun and basking in God's glory is a far preferable outcome to burning up and gnashing one's teeth in a fiery furnace.

1. Why do you think that Jesus keeps warning to "Wait and see how things turn out; you may be surprised"?

2. What do you think of the suggestion that there is a personal devil working woe in this world, just as there is a personal Savior leading people in the paths of righteousness for his name's sake?

FIVE

The Parables of Treasure, Pearls, and the Net

Matthew 13:44–52 *"The kingdom of heaven is like treasure hidden in a field. When a man found it, he hid it again, and then in his joy went and sold all he had and bought that field.*

45"Again, the kingdom of heaven is like a merchant looking for fine pearls. 46When he found one of great value, he went away and sold everything he had and bought it.

47"Once again, the kingdom of heaven is like a net that was let down into the lake and caught all kinds of fish. 48When it was full, the fishermen pulled it up on the shore. Then they sat down and collected the good fish in baskets, but threw the bad away. 49This is how it will be at the end of the age. The angels will come and separate the wicked from the righteous 50and throw them into the blazing furnace, where there will be weeping and gnashing of teeth.

51"Have you understood all these things?" Jesus asked.

"Yes," they replied.

52He said to them, "Therefore every teacher of the law who has become a disciple in the kingdom of heaven is like the owner of a house who brings out of his storeroom new treasures as well as old."

Key Observation. The kingdom is so precious, and being part of it so important, that Jesus suggests it's like a treasure or pearl that one would give anything to possess.

Understanding the Word. All of these parables speak of something that is not evident, something that is hidden, which nonetheless is very valuable. In the case of the treasure in the field it is something discovered by accident, but the discoverer realizes its worth and gives everything up to purchase that field. In the case of the exquisite pearl, it was not buried, but it was also not something the person expected to find. Both of those brief parables end the same with the person selling everything in order to obtain the prized possession. Jesus here is explaining just how valuable the kingdom and being part of it really is. There is nothing more valuable, more important, more needed, more precious. Jesus is suggesting that one should be prepared to risk everything in order to be in the kingdom, part of Jesus' community.

The parable of the net is somewhat different, except that it is not immediately obvious which are the good fish and which are the bad ones. Again, the suggestion is made that the community of Christ is a mixed multitude and it will not be sorted out until the end of the age who counts as a good fish and who does not. And notice it is the angels' job, not human beings, to do the sorting out of things in the end times. Again, we are told to leave judgment in the hands of God, as the Sermon on the Mount already suggested. The last parable indicates that being good or bad in this life determines whether one gets a good or bad outcome in the life to come as well. Not merely the world, but the church will be sifted when Christ returns.

1. Which elements in these parables do you find most challenging?

2. Which features of these parables seem most comforting?

WEEK FIVE

GATHERING DISCUSSION OUTLINE

A. Open session in prayer. Ask that God would astonish us anew with fresh insight from His Word and transform us into the disciples that Jesus desires us to become.

B. View video for this week's readings.

C. What were key insights or takeaways that you gained from your reading during the week and from watching the video commentary? In particular, how did these help you to grow in your faith and understanding of Scripture? What parts of the Bible lesson or study raised questions for you?

D. Discuss questions selected from the daily readings.

1. **KEY OBSERVATION:** Jesus used parables for his public teaching to the crowds.

    DISCUSSION QUESTION: What type of soil are you? How would you need to change in order to be good soil consistently?

2. **KEY OBSERVATION:** Jesus spoke in parables to convey to the crowds that their hearts were hard and, unless they repented and turned to him, they would not understand his message.

    DISCUSSION QUESTION: What role does repentance and turning to God play in helping a person understand God's Word?

3. **KEY OBSERVATION:** Jesus explains the parable to encourage his disciples, but also to give a warning about obstacles to discipleship.

DISCUSSION QUESTION: What obstacles hinder you the most in your following of Jesus—anxieties about life, persecution, or the desire for great wealth?

4. **KEY OBSERVATION:** Jesus warns that disciples can't fully identify kingdom people until the kingdom fully comes on earth and God separates the wheat from the weeds.

   DISCUSSION QUESTION: Why do you think that Jesus keeps warning to "Wait and see how things turn out; you may be surprised"?

5. **KEY OBSERVATION:** The kingdom is so precious, and being part of it so important, that Jesus suggests it's like a treasure or pearl that one would give anything to possess.

   DISCUSSION QUESTION: Which elements in these parables do you find most challenging?

E. As the study concludes, consider specific ways that this week's Bible lesson invites us to grow and calls us to change. How do this week's scriptures call us to think differently? How do they challenge us to change in order to align ourselves with God's work in the world? What specific actions should we take to apply the insights of the lesson into our daily lives? What kind of person does our Bible lesson call us to become?

F. Close session with prayer. Emphasize God's ongoing work of transformation in our lives in preparation for loving mission and service in the world. Pray for missing class members as well as for persons whom we need to invite to join our study.

Matthew 14–17

The Peter Principle

ONE

Jesus and Peter Walk on Water

Matthew 14:22–36 *Immediately Jesus made the disciples get into the boat and go on ahead of him to the other side, while he dismissed the crowd. ²³After he had dismissed them, he went up on a mountainside by himself to pray. Later that night, he was there alone, ²⁴and the boat was already a considerable distance from land, buffeted by the waves because the wind was against it.*

²⁵Shortly before dawn Jesus went out to them, walking on the lake. ²⁶When the disciples saw him walking on the lake, they were terrified. "It's a ghost," they said, and cried out in fear.

²⁷But Jesus immediately said to them: "Take courage! It is I. Don't be afraid." ²⁸"Lord, if it's you," Peter replied, "tell me to come to you on the water." ²⁹"Come," he said.

Then Peter got down out of the boat, walked on the water and came toward Jesus. ³⁰But when he saw the wind, he was afraid and, beginning to sink, cried out, "Lord, save me!"

³¹Immediately Jesus reached out his hand and caught him. "You of little faith," he said, "why did you doubt?"

³²And when they climbed into the boat, the wind died down. ³³Then those who were in the boat worshiped him, saying, "Truly you are the Son of God."

³⁴When they had crossed over, they landed at Gennesaret. ³⁵And when the men of that place recognized Jesus, they sent word to all the surrounding country. People brought all their sick to him ³⁶and begged him to let the sick just touch the edge of his cloak, and all who touched it were healed.

Key Observation. Risk-taking is required to be a person of faith. Say what you will about Peter's mistakes and failures, at least he was prepared to get out of the boat and try to come to Jesus.

Understanding the Word. The story of Jesus walking on the water appears in all the Gospels. It is clear that Matthew wants to highlight the trials and triumphs of Peter in a way that is not the case in other Gospels. In this Gospel alone not only do we have this episode involving Jesus and Peter, but we also have the unique saying about Jesus building his church on Peter (16:18–19), the episode where Jesus tells Peter to go fishing for the temple tax coin (17:24–28), and the question of Peter about how many times one should forgive one's brother (18:21). Clearly this writer desires to present a full-orbed picture of Peter. Perhaps it is because this Gospel was likely written for Jewish Christians.

A few points are important to understanding this story. First, early Jews didn't much like large bodies of water. They were not a sea-going people. They associated water with chaos and instability. They also believed that the spirits of the dead, in particular those who died on a lake or at sea and were not properly buried, dwelt in bodies of water. So when the water was stirred, a spirit might show up from the deep. This is precisely what the disciples assume when they first see Jesus through the storm at a distance.

Second, Jesus reassures the disciples saying, "It's just me, don't be afraid." Peter responds, "If it's you, then tell me to come to you on the water," and Jesus says, "Come." In other words, Peter is being brave, and quite literally taking a step out of the boat on faith. We, however, should be careful what we promise. We learn something about ourselves when our faith is tested in a crisis or under pressure, and many a person who is brave before the storm, is not so brave or calm during the storm. However, none of the other disciples even attempt what Peter does, and so while Peter may earn the epithet "O ye of little faith" here, what does that say about the other men in the boat? At least Peter shows faith.

But why did he sink? The text says it is because he saw the great wind and became afraid. In the Gospels, the opposite of fear is not primarily courage, but rather faith, and when fear overwhelms one's faith bad things happen. Doubts happen. A lack of trust in God happens. In any case, Peter cries out for Jesus to rescue him (which is what "save" means in this story), and he does so.

Why, then, does the story end with the disciples worshiping Jesus and proclaiming him the divine Son of God? Presumably this is because they know the Old Testament stories. For instance, they know the psalms where you have the dramatic images of God coming on the water or controlling the storms and wind, and the like. If Jesus can do that, then Jesus must be part of the divine identity.

1. Do you suppose if you had been in the same boat with these disciples you would have acted more like Peter or more like the rest of those in the boat?

2. What do we learn about faith under duress from this story?

TWO

The Faith of a Canaanite Woman

Matthew 15:21–28 *Leaving that place, Jesus withdrew to the region of Tyre and Sidon. ²²A Canaanite woman from that vicinity came to him, crying out, "Lord, Son of David, have mercy on me! My daughter is demon-possessed and suffering terribly."*

²³Jesus did not answer a word. So his disciples came to him and urged him, "Send her away, for she keeps crying out after us."

²⁴He answered, "I was sent only to the lost sheep of Israel."

²⁵The woman came and knelt before him. "Lord, help me!" she said.

²⁶He replied, "It is not right to take the children's bread and toss it to the dogs."

²⁷"Yes it is, Lord," she said. "Even the dogs eat the crumbs that fall from their master's table."

²⁸Then Jesus said to her, "Woman, you have great faith! Your request is granted." And her daughter was healed at that moment.

Key Observation. Trusting Jesus doesn't seem to be the exclusive trait of a disciple. Even outsiders can have a strong faith in Jesus.

Understanding the Word. One of the interesting things that happens when you compare the Markan version of this story (Mark 7:24–30) with the one here in Matthew is that while Matthew calls the woman in question a Canaanite woman, Mark calls her a Syrophonecian woman. They are both correct, but the term Mark uses shows us that his audience must be in the western part of the Roman Empire, probably Rome itself, for only westerners spoke of Syrian Phoenicians. This is outsider language, whereas "Canaanite" is the old Jewish term for people who lived in or near the promised land but were not Jews.

On the surface, Jesus appears to be harsh with the woman who is desperate to have her daughter exorcised. But notice that the disciples first complain, "Send her away because she's annoying us with her pleading." They had already turned a deaf ear to her lament. In that context, Jesus' word, "I was sent only to the lost sheep of Israel," could be an attempt by Jesus to let the disciples hear how cold-hearted they sounded. After all, why had Jesus left Israel to go to the region of Tyre and Sidon in the first place if he didn't intend to do any ministry there? He certainly wasn't on vacation. Perhaps, then, Jesus is testing both the compassion of the disciples and the faith of the woman at the same time. If so, the disciples fail the test, but the woman succeeds and wins the healing she wants for her daughter.

One other aspect of this is important. The metaphorical exchange between Jesus and the woman about bread and dogs can be interpreted in several ways. The question is whether the woman is saying, "Yes, Jesus, you are right that dogs have no right to the bread, but nevertheless help me out," or is her response to Jesus, "Oh yes it is, because even the dogs eat with the children when the crumbs fall from the table"? Regardless, the woman is not commended for being clever or having a clever retort, but rather for her great faith. She will not give up until she achieves her goal, unlike Peter, who never reaches Jesus. Mark does not have the disciples complaining about the woman, nor the remark of Jesus to let the children eat first, so it seems clear that the Matthean version of the story is meant to contrast the Israelite disciples who are just annoyed with a pagan woman's great faith.

1. Does your reading of this story suggest that Jesus was being too hard on the woman? If not, why not?

2. What is the lesson here for understanding God's mission? Who are outsiders in your world?

THREE

Peter Declares Jesus the Messiah; Jesus Declares the Son of Man Must Die

Matthew 16:13–28 *When Jesus came to the region of Caesarea Philippi, he asked his disciples, "Who do people say the Son of Man is?"*

[14]They replied, "Some say John the Baptist; others say Elijah; and still others, Jeremiah or one of the prophets."

[15]"But what about you?" he asked. "Who do you say I am?"

[16]Simon Peter answered, "You are the Messiah, the Son of the living God."

[17]Jesus replied, "Blessed are you, Simon son of Jonah, for this was not revealed to you by flesh and blood, but by my Father in heaven. [18]And I tell you that you are Peter, and on this rock I will build my church, and the gates of Hades will not overcome it. [19]I will give you the keys of the kingdom of heaven; whatever you bind on earth will be bound in heaven, and whatever you loose on earth will be loosed in heaven." [20]Then he ordered his disciples not to tell anyone that he was the Messiah.

[21]From that time on Jesus began to explain to his disciples that he must go to Jerusalem and suffer many things at the hands of the elders, the chief priests and the teachers of the law, and that he must be killed and on the third day be raised to life.

[22]Peter took him aside and began to rebuke him. "Never, Lord!" he said. "This shall never happen to you!"

[23]Jesus turned and said to Peter, "Get behind me, Satan! You are a stumbling block to me; you do not have in mind the concerns of God, but merely human concerns."

[24]Then Jesus said to his disciples, "Whoever wants to be my disciple must deny themselves and take up their cross and follow me. [25]For whoever wants to save their life will lose it, but whoever loses their life for me will find it. [26]What good will it be for someone to gain the whole world, yet forfeit their soul? Or what can anyone give in exchange for their soul? [27]For the Son of Man is going to come in his Father's glory with his angels, and then he will reward each person according to what they have done.

²⁸*"Truly I tell you, some who are standing here will not taste death before they see the Son of Man coming in his kingdom."*

Key Observation. Discipleship involves a radical commitment to follow Jesus at all costs into the world on mission.

Understanding the Word. This is a story where Peter goes from the penthouse to the outhouse in about five minutes flat. One minute he has uniquely discerned the true identity of Jesus and is commended for it. Jesus calls him a rock and says that he will build his community on the basis of such confessions. The next minute, after Jesus says the Son of Man must suffer and be killed, Peter exclaims, "No way!" and then Jesus calls Peter "Satan," someone getting in the way of his doing God's will and fulfilling his mission. It is quite a sudden change of fortunes.

As I mentioned, the context is crucial. The story takes place outside the Holy Land in the territory of Herod Philip, yet another son of Herod the Great. But, more important, the city that Philip renamed Caesarea Philippi, after Caesar and himself, was originally the Greek city of Banyas, or Panyas, and it was full of statues of pagan deities and "sons of the gods." In particular, it had a temple to the Emperor Augustus who was worshiped as a god. It is in this context that Jesus chose to reveal his identity, in contrast to those phony sons of gods. As my friend Tom Wright likes to say, "Jesus is the reality of which Caesar and these other so-called gods are parodies."

Jesus says to Peter that he could not have deduced Jesus' identity by pure logic or process of elimination. There were guesses that Jesus was another prophet like that greatest of northern prophets Elijah, or perhaps like Jeremiah. Jesus was indeed a prophet, but he was so much more than that, and Peter correctly identifies what that "more" was. But Jesus tells him that it was a revelation that caused him to have this insight.

There has been endless debate about what is meant by "and on this rock I will build my church, and the gates of Hades will not overcome it" (16:18). The short answer is probably that Jesus is commending Peter's affirmation of faith; it will be the basis of his new community, not some ethnic criterion. As for the second half of the saying, in Banyas/Caesarea Philippi and right next to all the niches with the statues of pagan gods was the cave of Pan, and it was believed that the stream that came forth from the cave led down into the

70

underworld (not to be confused with the later Jewish and Christian idea of hell). The underworld is just the land of the dead in Greco-Roman thinking. It's where everyone goes when they die, with the possible exception of great heroes like Hercules who may be taken up into the realm of the gods, or great war heroes who may end up in Elysium, the paradise islands in the next life. In other words, Jesus is saying that his community will never die out—period! This is good news for those living in times when the church is declining or under persecution.

Immediately, Jesus predicts his suffering and death (16:21). This shocks Peter. No one was looking for a crucified Messiah. In the Markan presentation of this story, Mark is suggesting that until you know who Jesus really is, you can't understand why he must die on the cross. Matthew may have something similar in mind, but clearly Peter does not get the message about the coming demise of Jesus, and strongly objects. But what this story also suggests is that it was indeed a temptation for Jesus to avoid the cross. We see this clearly in the garden of Gethsemane story (see Matthew 26:36–45) where Jesus prays that the cup might pass from him, but it does not. Jesus doesn't say "crucified" here, he simply says "killed" (16:21). Perhaps Jesus first understood he would be martyred, but only later understood this would involve the most hideous means of ancient execution: crucifixion. The final verse in this passage seems to refer to the following story about the transfiguration, which is a preview of Jesus' second coming. The three disciples will get this preview.

1. How have you reacted in life when you had an "oh yes!" and an "oh no!" experience back-to-back? Can you identify with Peter?

2. How does the context of Matthew 16 illuminate its meaning?

FOUR

The Transfiguration

Matthew 17:1–13 *After six days Jesus took with him Peter, James and John the brother of James, and led them up a high mountain by themselves. ²There he was transfigured before them. His face shone like the sun, and his clothes became as white as the light. ³Just then there appeared before them Moses and Elijah, talking with Jesus.*

⁴Peter said to Jesus, "Lord, it is good for us to be here. If you wish, I will put up three shelters—one for you, one for Moses and one for Elijah."

⁵While he was still speaking, a bright cloud covered them, and a voice from the cloud said, "This is my Son, whom I love; with him I am well pleased. Listen to him!"

⁶When the disciples heard this, they fell facedown to the ground, terrified. ⁷But Jesus came and touched them. "Get up," he said. "Don't be afraid." ⁸When they looked up, they saw no one except Jesus.

⁹As they were coming down the mountain, Jesus instructed them, "Don't tell anyone what you have seen, until the Son of Man has been raised from the dead."

¹⁰The disciples asked him, "Why then do the teachers of the law say that Elijah must come first?"

¹¹Jesus replied, "To be sure, Elijah comes and will restore all things. ¹²But I tell you, Elijah has already come, and they did not recognize him, but have done to him everything they wished. In the same way, the Son of Man is going to suffer at their hands." ¹³Then the disciples understood that he was talking to them about John the Baptist.

Key Observation. The transfiguration reveals the glorious character and identity of Jesus, but the disciples once again fail to grasp its meaning.

Understanding the Word. Some of life's peak experiences are not fully understood or appreciated until after the fact. This was clearly the case with the disciples and the transfiguration experience. It needs to be understood from the outset that this event is not a preview of the resurrection, but rather of the return of the Son of Man in glory. Nothing in this story suggests that the disciples didn't recognize Jesus during the transfiguration, but that is an issue in the resurrection stories. By contrast, when the Son of Man returns in glory, everyone will recognize who he is.

What is the function of this story, which only involves Jesus and the three disciples? The point seems to be to hammer home to the three that Jesus is indeed the Son of God (something they already affirmed on the lake when Jesus walked on water) and that they need to pay strict attention to what Jesus is saying. What about the appearance of Elijah and Moses, the representatives of the prophets and the Law? Luke, in his account of this story (Luke 9:18–36), tells us they were talking with Jesus about his exodus, that is, his leaving of the earth. Elijah was taken up in a chariot into heaven, whereas early Jews also believed that Moses was taken up into heaven.

But what in the world is Peter suggesting when he offers to Jesus to build three shelters for the three celestial figures? In Mark's account in 9:2–13, he comments, "He did not know what to say, for they were terrified" (v. 6 NRSV). Apparently, Peter thought like ancient Hebrews that there should be some shrine or commemoration of the spot where the holy ones appeared like at Bethel. It must be remembered that ancient people thought that high places on mountains were where you encountered divine beings, and where they built their shrines and sanctuaries. In any case, Jesus doesn't want the disciples discussing this until after he is raised from the dead, but alas, they don't even understand what Jesus means by that yet!

1. How do you think you would have reacted if Christ had suddenly appeared to you in glorious form as he did here?

2. What is the meaning of the transfiguration and how does it serve to encourage disciples?

FIVE

Jesus Tells Peter, "Go Fishing"

Matthew 17:24–27 *After Jesus and his disciples arrived in Capernaum, the collectors of the two-drachma temple tax came to Peter and asked, "Doesn't your teacher pay the temple tax?"*

25"Yes, he does," he replied.

When Peter came into the house, Jesus was the first to speak. "What do you think, Simon?" he asked. "From whom do the kings of the earth collect duty and taxes—from their own children or from others?"

26"From others," Peter answered.

"Then the children are exempt," Jesus said to him. 27"But so that we may not cause offense, go to the lake and throw out your line. Take the first fish you catch; open its mouth and you will find a four-drachma coin. Take it and give it to them for my tax and yours."

Key Observation. As children of the Great King, God's people have privileges, but the key principal for missional living is to avoid exercising our rights if they cause offense and obscure our sharing of the gospel.

Understanding the Word. There were a variety of taxes that Jews were expected to pay, and they should not all be lumped together. The temple tax had to do with supporting the temple in Jerusalem and was not a Roman tax. It had existed from before the Roman appearance in Judea. In addition, there were tolls collected on borders between Galilee and the surrounding regions. This was a tax by regional authorities, and in addition there were regular taxes collected by Herod Antipas for himself and his realm, but also the Romans had to be paid, particularly in Judea where the "render unto Caesar" issue is raised. Judea was a Roman province, Galilee was not; it was ruled by a client king.

It is not clear whether this story is meant to be humorous or serious; it could be either or both. In any case, Peter would be paying the temple tax not out of his own pocket, but out of money he found in the lake! Notice that in Jerusalem Jesus commends the widow for giving her two widow's mites into the temple treasury (see Mark 12:41–44; Luke 21:1–4). This may be a reference as well to the temple tax, or it may be a reference to the tithe. In any case, Jesus is not opposed to his followers paying taxes to whomever taxes are due, and Paul in Romans 13 agrees with this view. When Peter, in 1 Peter 3:17, says, "honor the emperor," he may be alluding to paying taxes as well. Notice, finally, that Jesus himself is said to pay the temple tax, setting the example. This story and the other related ones do not encourage us as Jesus' disciples to grumble about paying taxes to whom taxes are due. The key is not to cause offense among those whom we are called to proclaim the gospel.

1. What is your attitude about paying taxes?

2. What rights do we need to choose not to exploit for the sake of sharing the gospel with others today?

WEEK SIX

GATHERING DISCUSSION OUTLINE

A. Open session in prayer. Ask that God would astonish us anew with fresh insight from his Word and transform us into the disciples that Jesus desires us to become.

B. View video for this week's readings.

C. What were key insights or takeaways that you gained from your reading during the week and from watching the video commentary? In particular, how did these help you to grow in your faith and understanding of Scripture? What parts of the Bible lesson or study raised questions for you?

D. Discuss questions selected from the daily readings.

   1. **KEY OBSERVATION:** Risk-taking is required to be a person of faith. Say what you will about Peter's mistakes and failures, at least he was prepared to get out of the boat and try to come to Jesus.

   DISCUSSION QUESTION: What do we learn about faith under duress from this story?

   2. **KEY OBSERVATION:** Trusting Jesus doesn't seem to be the exclusive trait of a disciple. Even outsiders can have a strong faith in Jesus.

   DISCUSSION QUESTION: What is the lesson here for understanding God's mission? Who are outsiders in your world?

   3. **KEY OBSERVATION:** Discipleship involves a radical commitment to follow Jesus at all costs into the world on mission.

DISCUSSION QUESTION: How have you reacted in life when you had an "oh yes!" and an "oh no!" experience back-to-back? Can you identify with Peter?

4. **KEY OBSERVATION:** The transfiguration reveals the glorious character and identity of Jesus, but the disciples once again fail to grasp its meaning.

   DISCUSSION QUESTION: How do you think you would have reacted if Christ had suddenly appeared to you in glorious form as he did here?

5. **KEY OBSERVATION:** As children of the Great King, God's people have privileges, but the key principal for missional living is to avoid exercising our rights if they cause offense and obscure our sharing of the gospel.

   DISCUSSION QUESTION: What rights do we need to choose not to exploit for the sake of sharing the gospel with others today?

E. As the study concludes, consider specific ways that this week's Bible lesson invites us to grow and calls us to change. How do this week's scriptures call us to think differently? How do they challenge us to change in order to align ourselves with God's work in the world? What specific actions should we take to apply the insights of the lesson into our daily lives? What kind of person does our Bible lesson call us to become?

F. Close session with prayer. Emphasize God's ongoing work of transformation in our lives in preparation for loving mission and service in the world. Pray for missing class members as well as for persons whom we need to invite to join our study.

WEEK SEVEN

Matthew 18–20

Forgiveness, Impediments to Following, Parables

ONE

Forgiveness and the Parable of the Unmerciful Servant

Matthew 18:21–35 *Then Peter came to Jesus and asked, "Lord, how many times shall I forgive my brother or sister who sins against me? Up to seven times?"* ²²*Jesus answered, "I tell you, not seven times, but seventy-seven times.*

²³*"Therefore, the kingdom of heaven is like a king who wanted to settle accounts with his servants.* ²⁴*As he began the settlement, a man who owed him ten thousand bags of gold was brought to him.* ²⁵*Since he was not able to pay, the master ordered that he and his wife and his children and all that he had be sold to repay the debt.*

²⁶*"At this the servant fell on his knees before him. 'Be patient with me,' he begged, 'and I will pay back everything.'* ²⁷*The servant's master took pity on him, canceled the debt and let him go.*

²⁸*"But when that servant went out, he found one of his fellow servants who owed him a hundred silver coins. He grabbed him and began to choke him. 'Pay back what you owe me!' he demanded.*

²⁹*"His fellow servant fell to his knees and begged him, 'Be patient with me, and I will pay it back.'*

³⁰*"But he refused. Instead, he went off and had the man thrown into prison until he could pay the debt.* ³¹*When the other servants saw what had happened, they were outraged and went and told their master everything that had happened.*

³²*"Then the master called the servant in. 'You wicked servant,' he said, 'I canceled all that debt of yours because you begged me to.* ³³*Shouldn't you have had mercy on your fellow servant just as I had on you?'* ³⁴*In anger his master handed him over to the jailers to be tortured, until he should pay back all he owed.*

³⁵*"This is how my heavenly Father will treat each of you unless you forgive your brother or sister from your heart."*

Key Observation. Jesus' gospel calls for the forgiveness of others.

Understanding the Word. A very different sort of context is required to understand what is going on in Matthew 18:21–22. Peter, apparently thinking he is generous, asks Jesus if it is sufficient to forgive his brother (which may mean his fellow Jew or, more specifically, his fellow follower of Jesus), seven times. Jesus says, "not seven times, but seventy-seven times," by which Jesus was attempting to refuse to limit forgiveness to a finite number. The number seven in Judaism was symbolic of perfection, and so doubtless Peter thought he was doing well, but Jesus responds with seventy-seven times, which probably means "keep on forgiving."

Now what is so telling about this is that Jesus' choice of number echoes just one Old Testament text, Genesis 4:24 (NRSV): "If Cain is avenged sevenfold, truly Lamech seventy-sevenfold," spoken by Lamech himself. Lamech is carrying on the killing activity of Cain, as an act of revenge. Jesus, by contrast, came to reverse the effects of human fallenness and wickedness. He came to reverse the curse on humanity. The way to break the cycle of violence is to simply forgive the person who has wronged you. Jesus' ethic was indeed an ethic of non-violence, but that says too little. It was an ethic of forgiveness and even love of one's enemy. While the behavior of Lamech sadly seems far more normal than the behavior and beliefs of Jesus, Jesus was serious about this ethic and paid the price for it. He showed the greater love by laying down his life as a ransom for all the others, even the most notorious sinners. One may think this is not natural behavior for a fallen human being, and that is correct. But Jesus believes that by God's love and grace a person can live out such an ethic. It may not be natural, but it is possible with the help of the Spirit.

The parable that follows Peter and Jesus' dialogue about forgiveness focuses on the forgiveness of a debt. It involves a king who forgives a servant's significant debt whom he is about to sell into slavery due to failure to repay a large sum—ten thousand talents (v. 24 NRSV), an astronomical amount he could never repay in a lifetime. Indeed, this poor servant owed the king more money than was likely in circulation in the whole country. The point is, the debt could never be paid; the only resolution was either punishment or forgiveness.

But though one might have expected gratitude from the forgiven servant, and a sense of what mercy is like, instead he goes out and tries to extract a small debt owed to him by a lesser servant of a mere one hundred denarii (v. 28 NRSV), a hundred days' wages, which is a miniscule amount compared to what the wicked servant owed. When the man couldn't pay, he threw the lesser servant in jail. But there would be justice. Word got back to the king about this and the king became very angry and had the man severely punished until he paid up.

What is the point of all this? One could say that the king represents God, and vengeance or payback should always be left in the hands of God, but our practice as followers of Jesus should be to always forgive. Perhaps the parable reassures that in the end no one will get away with injustice. But since Matthew 18:21–22 frames the discussion, surely the more positive point is the same one that is made in the Lord's Prayer: forgive us our debts/sins as we forgive our debtors/those who sin against us. There is some connection between our receiving forgiveness from God, and our willingness to forgive others as God forgives us. Put another way, unforgiveness puts an impediment in one's life to receiving forgiveness from God. There is a connection between vertical and horizontal forgiveness, just as there is a connection between love of God and of neighbor.

Finally, it should be stressed that forgiveness is one thing, liking a person or even being reconciled to a person is another. Forgiveness is necessary for a disciple of Jesus, but often it will not lead to reconciliation between the two parties. And one of the key reasons forgiveness is so necessary is that the one doing the forgiving needs to do it, as much as the one who has offended or harmed needs to receive it. Forgiveness offered is all one has control over. Whether it is received and embraced is another matter.

1. Why do you think Jesus made forgiveness such a crucial part of his message, even forgiving his tormentors when hanging on the cross?

2. Why is forgiveness often so difficult and costly to the one offering it?

TWO

The Problem with Riches

Matthew 19:16–30 *Just then a man came up to Jesus and asked, "Teacher, what good thing must I do to get eternal life?"*

17"Why do you ask me about what is good?" Jesus replied. "There is only One who is good. If you want to enter life, keep the commandments."

18"Which ones?" he inquired.

Jesus replied, "'You shall not murder, you shall not commit adultery, you shall not steal, you shall not give false testimony, 19 honor your father and mother,' and 'love your neighbor as yourself.'"

20"All these I have kept," the young man said. "What do I still lack?"

21Jesus answered, "If you want to be perfect, go, sell your possessions and give to the poor, and you will have treasure in heaven. Then come, follow me."

22When the young man heard this, he went away sad, because he had great wealth.

23Then Jesus said to his disciples, "Truly I tell you, it is hard for someone who is rich to enter the kingdom of heaven. 24Again I tell you, it is easier for a camel to go through the eye of a needle than for someone who is rich to enter the kingdom of God." rock entrance?

25When the disciples heard this, they were greatly astonished and asked, "Who then can be saved?"

26Jesus looked at them and said, "With man this is impossible, but with God all things are possible."

27Peter answered him, "We have left everything to follow you! What then will there be for us?"

28Jesus said to them, "Truly I tell you, at the renewal of all things, when the Son of Man sits on his glorious throne, you who have followed me will also sit on twelve thrones, judging the twelve tribes of Israel. 29And everyone who has left houses or brothers or sisters or father or mother or wife or children or fields for my sake will receive a hundred times as much and will inherit eternal life. 30But many who are first will be last, and many who are last will be first."

Key Observation. What is impossible for humankind is indeed possible for God.

Understanding the Word. There are many warnings about the dangers of wealth in the teachings of Jesus, and also of his followers, including both Paul ("the love of money is a root of all kinds of evil" [1 Tim. 6:10]) and James (see James 1–2). Jesus, in this famous response to the rich young man, explains that riches can actually prevent one from entering the kingdom of God. What is going on with this teaching is the insistence that anything one values more highly than God, anything that one places one's trust in that is less than God, God will require it of that person. Jesus essentially says to the rich young man, "good for you that you've kept the major commandments, now go sell your possessions and give to the poor and come and follow me if you would be perfect." The young man fails this highest of tests of whether he is truly sold out to God or not. For anything that takes the place of God in someone's life, God will require of that person. Only God can be the ultimate concern in a believer's life. Everything else is secondary, and everything else must be sacrificed to keep it that way, if need be, if God demands it.

Peter once again speaks up for the various disciples and reminds Jesus they have given up everything to follow him—their occupations, their homes, their families. Jesus promises that in the kingdom they will receive an even greater and more permanent family.

One word about the context should be added in conclusion. Money in Jesus' world had negative associations because it bore the likeness of living rulers, who were often oppressors and enslavers of God's people. Unlike our money, which has dead presidents on it, ancient Roman money was propaganda for living rulers. This is, in part, why Jesus says one "cannot serve both God and money" (Matt. 6:24).

1. What was the young man's problem that Jesus addressed?

2. What talents or treasures do we withhold from God? What would it look like for us to offer these fully to Jesus today?

THREE

The Parable of the Workers in the Vineyard

Matthew 20:1–16 *"For the kingdom of heaven is like a landowner who went out early in the morning to hire workers for his vineyard. ²He agreed to pay them a denarius for the day and sent them into his vineyard.*

³"About nine in the morning he went out and saw others standing in the marketplace doing nothing. ⁴He told them, 'You also go and work in my vineyard, and I will pay you whatever is right.' ⁵So they went.

"He went out again about noon and about three in the afternoon and did the same thing. ⁶About five in the afternoon he went out and found still others standing around. He asked them, 'Why have you been standing here all day long doing nothing?'

⁷"'Because no one has hired us,' they answered.

"He said to them, 'You also go and work in my vineyard.'

⁸"When evening came, the owner of the vineyard said to his foreman, 'Call the workers and pay them their wages, beginning with the last ones hired and going on to the first.'

⁹"The workers who were hired about five in the afternoon came and each received a denarius. ¹⁰So when those came who were hired first, they expected to receive more. But each one of them also received a denarius. ¹¹When they received it, they began to grumble against the landowner. ¹²'These who were hired last worked only one hour,' they said, 'and you have made them equal to us who have borne the burden of the work and the heat of the day.'

¹³"But he answered one of them, 'I am not being unfair to you, friend. Didn't you agree to work for a denarius? ¹⁴Take your pay and go. I want to give the one who was hired last the same as I gave you. ¹⁵Don't I have the right to do what I want with my own money? Or are you envious because I am generous?'

¹⁶"So the last will be first, and the first will be last."

Key Observation. Mercy and compassion always go beyond mere fairness. Envy, however, is a sin.

Understanding the Word. This memorable parable talks about an owner of a vineyard who is in desperate need of getting his crop in on that day. To that end, he goes repeatedly to the town square to hire more and more day laborers to make sure the job gets done before the day's end. The normal day's wage is one denarius, and at the beginning of the parable this is what the owner promises to pay those he hires first. Those he hires second he promises to pay what is right without specifying. He makes no promises to those he hires at noon, three, and even five in the evening, only an hour before sundown. He pays the men at the end of the day in reverse order, giving even the man who worked only an hour a full denarius. This, however, set up an anticipation by those who worked longer that they would receive more, but it was not to be, and there was grumbling. The economic side of the story is that probably all the workers were in equal need of a full day's pay to feed their families, and the owner simply had compassion on those who did less. The irony is that the workers who have agreed to what is a fair wage, suddenly think it's not fair to be generous to others who worked less. But, in fact, fairness doesn't enter into the matter. It's a matter of grace and compassion. To the small-minded, forgiveness, grace, or generosity to those who have not fully earned what they get will always seem unfair but, in fact, it's not an injustice. The owner was fully just to all, and more than fair to some. But more than fair is never equal to unfair. Justice is when you get what you deserve. Mercy is when you are not given some negative thing that you deserve. Grace or compassion is when you are given something positive you have not earned or deserved.

1. What are God's standards when it comes to fairness?

2. What is the difference between justice and compassion?

FOUR

A Mother's Proud Request

Matthew 20:20–28 *Then the mother of Zebedee's sons came to Jesus with her sons and, kneeling down, asked a favor of him.*
  ²¹"What is it you want?" he asked.

She said, "Grant that one of these two sons of mine may sit at your right and the other at your left in your kingdom."

²²"You don't know what you are asking," Jesus said to them. "Can you drink the cup I am going to drink?"

"We can," they answered.

²³Jesus said to them, "You will indeed drink from my cup, but to sit at my right or left is not for me to grant. These places belong to those for whom they have been prepared by my Father."

²⁴When the ten heard about this, they were indignant with the two brothers. ²⁵Jesus called them together and said, "You know that the rulers of the Gentiles lord it over them, and their high officials exercise authority over them. ²⁶Not so with you. Instead, whoever wants to become great among you must be your servant, ²⁷and whoever wants to be first must be your slave—²⁸just as the Son of Man did not come to be served, but to serve, and to give his life as a ransom for many."

Key Observation. Servanthood is the mark of true greatness in the kingdom of heaven.

Understanding the Word. In Matthew's Gospel, Jesus routinely critiques the disciples' lack of faith and/or understanding. Although it is the sons of Zebedees's mother who requests a place of authority for her sons, Jesus addresses the brothers James and John directly. They have asked for what is not theirs to request. They, in essence, ask to be co-rulers with Jesus in his kingdom. But they do this without fully understanding or committing to the mission of Jesus. So in response, Jesus asks if they are prepared to be baptized with the same baptism coming his way (i.e., death), and they rather glibly say they are able (v. 22 KJV). In fact, it is true that Herod Agrippa did away with James son of Zebedee less than fifteen years after Jesus' death.

Jesus says that sort of thing is his Father's decision, not his own decision, and in any case, it's the wrong question. The better question would be: Who is willing to be the servant, not the one who is seated above them all? Needless to say, the ten are indignant at the two, but one wonders which of them were thinking, *Why didn't I ask for that privilege first?* But Jesus shames them all by saying it's not about seats of honor, it's about self-sacrificial service like Jesus gives on the cross. Servanthood is at the heart of the gospel. It is central to the message of the cross. Those who would be first will be last. Jesus did not come to lord power over others but to live sacrificially and surrender his life for the sake of the salvation of the world. In many ways, verse 28 is a profound summary of the gospel.

1. When does a desire for recognition and honor get in the way of being a self-sacrificial Christian person?

2. What are some specific ways that you model Jesus' ethic of servant-hood in your everyday life?

FIVE

Jesus Comes to Town

Matthew 21:1–11 *As they approached Jerusalem and came to Bethphage on the Mount of Olives, Jesus sent two disciples, ²saying to them, "Go to the village ahead of you, and at once you will find a donkey tied there, with her colt by her. Untie them and bring them to me. ³If anyone says anything to you, say that the Lord needs them, and he will send them right away."*

⁴This took place to fulfill what was spoken through the prophet:

⁵"Say to Daughter Zion, 'See, your king comes to you, gentle and riding on a donkey, and on a colt, the foal of a donkey.'"

⁶The disciples went and did as Jesus had instructed them. ⁷They brought the donkey and the colt and placed their cloaks on them for Jesus to sit on. ⁸A very large crowd spread their cloaks on the road, while others cut branches from the trees and spread them on the road. ⁹The crowds that went ahead of him and those that followed shouted, "Hosanna to the Son of David!" "Blessed is he who comes in the name of the Lord!" "Hosanna in the highest heaven!"

¹⁰When Jesus entered Jerusalem, the whole city was stirred and asked, "Who is this?"

¹¹The crowds answered, "This is Jesus, the prophet from Nazareth in Galilee."

Key Observation. When Jesus enters Jerusalem during Passover, it appears he is following a prophetic script to reveal who he is and what his intentions are.

Understanding the Word. Matthew's account of the triumphal entry does indeed show the disciples and crowds apparently honoring Jesus as he rides in on a donkey. By riding a donkey rather than a mature horse, he avoids the image of a returning war hero. But Jesus is not that sort of king. It seems likely that Jesus got his disciples to requisition the animal he rode from one of his local disciples in Bethany, namely, from the family of Lazarus, for the account says that all the disciples had to say was, "the master has need of it." The account mentions palm branches, and the waving of the palm branches was used to celebrate the Maccabean victory retaking Jerusalem.

It must be admitted that probably Jesus' riding in on the donkey, coupled with the pilgrims saying "Hosanna," then coupled with the palm branches raised all sorts of expectations about Jesus being some sort of new messianic or prophetic leader that might solve Jerusalem's problems, or even triumph over the Romans. But again, Jesus was not that sort of king and was not setting out to set up that sort of kingdom in Jerusalem. Notice, even with all the fanfare, that the end of the segment has the resident of Jerusalem asking who in the world is this exalted person, to which the crowd only answers, "Jesus, the prophet from Nazareth." They do not necessarily suggest he is the Messiah.

It is, however, possible that in the case of someone like Judas, if he had previously been a political zealot, that this entry signaled to him that Jesus would perhaps take over things in Jerusalem, and the cleansing of the temple (Matthew 21:12–13) might well have been interpreted as a symbolic gesture suggesting Jesus would clean house. But then when Jesus reiterates he came to die, not to start a coup, this must have crushed the hopes of anyone with zealot inclinations about kicking out the Romans. Perhaps that is why Judas does what he does at the end of the week.

Matthew is interested here, and in what follows in the Passion narrative, in emphasizing that what happened during this week was a fulfillment of one prophecy after another. Part of the reason for this is not just that Jesus did some unusual and unexpected things, but especially that no one was expecting a crucified Messiah, not even Jesus' disciples, despite what he kept telling them. Citing scriptures repeatedly is Matthew's way of saying this was God's plan all along, however much it did not meet the expectations of the crowds, the authorities, and even the disciples. Jesus did not come to meet their expectations or demands, but rather to do God's will, and God's will was that his Son fulfill the prophecies and ransom captive Israel. He also came to meet our needs.

1. How do the symbols of Jesus' entry provide clues to his mission and identity?

2. What is ironic about the expectations of the crowds and disciples? How does Jesus ultimately fulfill these expectations?

WEEK SEVEN

GATHERING DISCUSSION OUTLINE

A. Open session in prayer. Ask that God would astonish us anew with fresh insight from his Word and transform us into the disciples that Jesus desires us to become.

B. View video for this week's readings.

C. Ask: What were key insights or takeaways that you gained from your reading during the week and from watching the video commentary? In particular, how did these help you to grow in your faith and understanding of Scripture? What parts of the Bible lesson or study raised questions for you?

D. Discuss questions selected from the daily readings.

1. **KEY OBSERVATION:** Jesus' gospel calls for the forgiveness of others.

   DISCUSSION QUESTION: Why do you think Jesus made forgiveness such a crucial part of his message, even forgiving his tormentors when hanging on the cross?

2. **KEY OBSERVATION:** What is impossible for humankind is indeed possible for God.

   DISCUSSION QUESTION: What talents or treasures do we withhold from God? What would it look like for us to offer these fully to Jesus today?

3. **KEY OBSERVATION:** Mercy and compassion always go beyond mere fairness. Envy, however, is a sin.

   DISCUSSION QUESTION: What are God's standards when it comes to fairness?

4. **KEY OBSERVATION:** Servanthood is the mark of true greatness in the kingdom of heaven.

   DISCUSSION QUESTION: What are some specific ways that you model Jesus' ethic of servanthood in your everyday life?

5. **KEY OBSERVATION:** When Jesus enters Jerusalem during Passover, it appears he is following a prophetic script to reveal who he is and what his intentions are.

   DISCUSSION QUESTION: How do the symbols of Jesus' entry provide clues to his mission and identity?

E. As the study concludes, consider specific ways that this week's Bible lesson invites us to grow and calls us to change. How do this week's scriptures call us to think differently? How do they challenge us to change in order to align ourselves with God's work in the world? What specific actions should we take to apply the insights of the lesson into our daily lives? What kind of person does our Bible lesson call us to become?

F. Close session with prayer. Emphasize God's ongoing work of transformation in our lives in preparation for loving mission and service in the world. Pray for missing class members as well as for persons whom we need to invite to join our study.

Matthew 21–28

The Passion and Resurrection of the Christ

ONE

The Cleansing of the Temple and the Cursing of the Fig Tree

Matthew 21:12–22 *Jesus entered the temple courts and drove out all who were buying and selling there. He overturned the tables of the money changers and the benches of those selling doves.* [13]*"It is written," he said to them, "'My house will be called a house of prayer,' but you are making it 'a den of robbers.'"*

[14]*The blind and the lame came to him at the temple, and he healed them.* [15]*But when the chief priests and the teachers of the law saw the wonderful things he did and the children shouting in the temple courts, "Hosanna to the Son of David," they were indignant.*

[16]*"Do you hear what these children are saying?" they asked him.*

"Yes," replied Jesus, "have you never read,

"'From the lips of children and infants you, Lord, have called forth your praise'?"

[17]*And he left them and went out of the city to Bethany, where he spent the night.*

[18]*Early in the morning, as Jesus was on his way back to the city, he was hungry.* [19]*Seeing a fig tree by the road, he went up to it but found nothing on it except leaves. Then he said to it, "May you never bear fruit again!" Immediately the tree withered.*

[20]*When the disciples saw this, they were amazed. "How did the fig tree wither so quickly?" they asked.*

[21]Jesus replied, "Truly I tell you, if you have faith and do not doubt, not only can you do what was done to the fig tree, but also you can say to this mountain, 'Go, throw yourself into the sea,' and it will be done. [22]If you believe, you will receive whatever you ask for in prayer."

Key Observation. Understanding the relationship between the cursing of the fig tree and the cleansing of the temple is the key to understanding this passage.

Understanding the Word. Sometimes the stories of Jesus are so familiar that we overlook the signals in the text meant to convey their real significance. For example, this is not a story about a cleansing of the temple. Turning over tables and releasing a few animals wasn't going to transform the temple into what God intended it to be. Instead, Jesus' actions are a prophetic sign that signals some big event yet to come. In this case, the big event is the judgment on the temple, not the coming cleansing of the temple. The problem with the temple was that the hierarchy had turned a sacred venue into a money-making venue through the sale of animals. This would explain Jesus' partial quotation of Jeremiah 7:11 calling the temple a den of thieves.

But what is the connection between the action in the temple and the withering of the fig tree? Jesus curses the fig tree, and it instantly withers. But what is the fig tree a symbol of? Like the vine and the olive tree, all of these things are symbols of God's people, who are seen by Jesus as not bearing good fruit. I stress the words "good fruit" because there were spring male figs which, while somewhat bitter, were nonetheless edible (whereas the sweet female figs would be produced by the tree in the fall), but this tree had nothing but leaves even in April. It was sterile. And the disciples remark on how quickly the tree withered up. Both of these symbolic actions foreshadow the coming judgment on the temple and on God's people in AD 70. We must never forget that religion and politics were inherently intertwined, and a political or military judgment on Jerusalem was also viewed as a religious judgment from God.

One other little vignette is worth remarking on. In this account, Jesus does some healing in the temple for which he is praised by children, but this angers various temple officials. In other words, Jesus did not just foreshadow judgment on the temple, he also brought good news and healing to the temple during his last visit. This no doubt confused many there as to what his purpose and intentions were. Notice again that Jesus is called "Son of David" (v. 15) in response to his healings, which, as we have noted before, is an allusion to Solomon who was thought to have the wisdom of cures, and so Jesus is seen as one like Solomon.

1. How does the withering of the fig tree serve as an interpretation of Jesus' actions in the temple?

2. What do Jesus' actions in the temple teach us today?

T W O

The Last Supper and the Last Prayer

Matthew 26:17–46 *On the first day of the Festival of Unleavened Bread, the disciples came to Jesus and asked, "Where do you want us to make preparations for you to eat the Passover?"*

[18]He replied, "Go into the city to a certain man and tell him, 'The Teacher says: My appointed time is near. I am going to celebrate the Passover with my disciples at your house.'" [19]So the disciples did as Jesus had directed them and prepared the Passover.

[20]When evening came, Jesus was reclining at the table with the Twelve. [21]And while they were eating, he said, "Truly I tell you, one of you will betray me."

[22]They were very sad and began to say to him one after the other, "Surely you don't mean me, Lord?"

[23]Jesus replied, "The one who has dipped his hand into the bowl with me will betray me. [24]The Son of Man will go just as it is written about him. But woe to that man who betrays the Son of Man! It would be better for him if he had not been born."

[25]Then Judas, the one who would betray him, said, "Surely you don't mean me, Rabbi?"

Jesus answered, "You have said so."

[26]While they were eating, Jesus took bread, and when he had given thanks, he broke it and gave it to his disciples, saying, "Take and eat; this is my body."

[27]Then he took a cup, and when he had given thanks, he gave it to them, saying, "Drink from it, all of you. [28]This is my blood of the covenant, which is

poured out for many for the forgiveness of sins. ²⁹I tell you, I will not drink from this fruit of the vine from now on until that day when I drink it new with you in my Father's kingdom."

³⁰When they had sung a hymn, they went out to the Mount of Olives.

³¹Then Jesus told them, "This very night you will all fall away on account of me, for it is written: 'I will strike the shepherd, and the sheep of the flock will be scattered.'

³²"But after I have risen, I will go ahead of you into Galilee."

³³Peter replied, "Even if all fall away on account of you, I never will."

³⁴"Truly I tell you," Jesus answered, "this very night, before the rooster crows, you will disown me three times."

³⁵But Peter declared, "Even if I have to die with you, I will never disown you." And all the other disciples said the same.

³⁶Then Jesus went with his disciples to a place called Gethsemane, and he said to them, "Sit here while I go over there and pray." ³⁷He took Peter and the two sons of Zebedee along with him, and he began to be sorrowful and troubled. ³⁸Then he said to them, "My soul is overwhelmed with sorrow to the point of death. Stay here and keep watch with me."

³⁹Going a little farther, he fell with his face to the ground and prayed, "My Father, if it is possible, may this cup be taken from me. Yet not as I will, but as you will."

⁴⁰Then he returned to his disciples and found them sleeping. "Couldn't you men keep watch with me for one hour?" he asked Peter. ⁴¹"Watch and pray so that you will not fall into temptation. The spirit is willing, but the flesh is weak."

⁴²He went away a second time and prayed, "My Father, if it is not possible for this cup to be taken away unless I drink it, may your will be done."

⁴³When he came back, he again found them sleeping, because their eyes were heavy. ⁴⁴So he left them and went away once more and prayed the third time, saying the same thing.

⁴⁵Then he returned to the disciples and said to them, "Are you still sleeping and resting? Look, the hour has come, and the Son of Man is delivered into the hands of sinners. ⁴⁶Rise! Let us go! Here comes my betrayer!"

Key Observation. Jesus shows that sometimes doing God's will is the opposite of what one wants to do, but submission to God's will is necessary and, in the end, beneficial.

Understanding the Word. There seems little doubt that the last supper of Jesus was intended to be a Passover meal. The Passover meal, or *pesah,* was full of symbolism. The unleavened bread represented the haste with which the Hebrews had to leave Egypt when God set them free after the angel of death had "passed over" the Hebrew doors that had blood over them. Clearly enough, Jesus is reinterpreting and not merely celebrating the Passover when he says, "this is my body" or "this is my blood of the covenant" (vv. 26, 28). In neither case is he speaking literally nor is he talking about some sort of transformation of ordinary elements into his actual body and blood. There was little precedent in any case for thinking of a human death as a sacrifice for sins in early Judaism. My point is this—the Last Supper, which is the basis for the Lord's Supper, is a symbolic meal, not a meal where elements are transformed into something they previously were not. What is most remarkable is that Jesus is so confident that his coming death will benefit the disciples that *in advance of dying* he symbolically explains the benefits of this.

There is a little hint that Jesus expects to show up again after his demise; namely, he says he won't drink the fruit of the vine again until he drinks it new in the kingdom. There is also the promise that Jesus will go before them into Galilee after the coming debacle, and they can meet him there.

The emphasis is again on Peter in this account. Peter swears that even if all fall away he will not, and Peter accompanies Jesus when he goes off to pray in the garden of Gethsemane. Yet Peter does deny Jesus three times, in one of which he swears an oath to God that he does not know Jesus! It is a terrible thing to swear to God you don't know his Son.

Jesus' emotions are clear. He is deeply sorrowful that the disciples are all going to fall away, and he is saddened about having to give up his life as well. But it is not just any death that concerns him, but a death described as "drinking a cup," and this image from the Old Testament is one of undergoing the wrath of God on sin (see Isaiah 51:17; Jeremiah 25:17ff.; Ezekiel 23:31ff.). Jesus understands that he will be like the scapegoat, suffering the judgment of God on sin in the place of all the others. The irony, of course, is that Jesus is the one person who should not undergo such a judgment since he was without sin. He did not die for his sins, but rather for everyone else's.

Jesus' prayer to God in the garden echoes the Lord's Prayer from the Sermon on the Mount (Matthew 6:9–13). He addresses God as Father and speaks of God's will being done, even though he would prefer a different outcome. Matthew portrays the sorrowful Jesus as the righteous sufferer of the Psalms (e.g., Psalm 55:4–5). This story is a cautionary tale reminding us that God's love does not make God's people immune to bad experiences. What he does promise is to always be with us through those times. Jesus' life models this.

The disciples, even Peter, are not able to watch with Jesus as he prays through the night; they fail him in even this task. Thankfully, Jesus did not fail them.

1. How are the disciples (especially Peter) portrayed in these verses? What lessons or warnings can we draw for modern-day disciples?

2. How does Jesus view his coming death based on what he says at the Last Supper and in the garden?

THREE

Jesus before Pilate

Matthew 27:11–26 *Meanwhile Jesus stood before the governor, and the governor asked him, "Are you the king of the Jews?"*

"You have said so," Jesus replied.

¹²When he was accused by the chief priests and the elders, he gave no answer.

¹³Then Pilate asked him, "Don't you hear the testimony they are bringing against you?" ¹⁴But Jesus made no reply, not even to a single charge—to the great amazement of the governor.

¹⁵Now it was the governor's custom at the festival to release a prisoner chosen by the crowd. ¹⁶At that time they had a well-known prisoner whose name was Jesus Barabbas. ¹⁷So when the crowd had gathered, Pilate asked them, "Which one do you want me to release to you: Jesus Barabbas, or Jesus who is called the Messiah?" ¹⁸For he knew it was out of self-interest that they had handed Jesus over to him.

¹⁹While Pilate was sitting on the judge's seat, his wife sent him this message: "Don't have anything to do with that innocent man, for I have suffered a great deal today in a dream because of him."

²⁰*But the chief priests and the elders persuaded the crowd to ask for Barabbas and to have Jesus executed.*
²¹*"Which of the two do you want me to release to you?" asked the governor.*
"Barabbas," they answered.
²²*"What shall I do, then, with Jesus who is called the Messiah?" Pilate asked.*
They all answered, "Crucify him!"
²³*"Why? What crime has he committed?" asked Pilate.*
But they shouted all the louder, "Crucify him!"
²⁴*When Pilate saw that he was getting nowhere, but that instead an uproar was starting, he took water and washed his hands in front of the crowd. "I am innocent of this man's blood," he said. "It is your responsibility!"*
²⁵*All the people answered, "His blood is on us and on our children!"*
²⁶*Then he released Barabbas to them. But he had Jesus flogged, and handed him over to be crucified.*

Key Observation. Although Jesus stood before the Jewish authorities in Matthew 26:57–68, the Roman governor Pilate is the one ultimately responsible for condemning Jesus to death.

Understanding the Word. There are many mysteries about this account, and we will not be able to unpack them all here. Pilate asks Jesus if he is the Jewish king, and Jesus replies, "You have said so." But, in fact, Jesus' opaque response could be a more positive one if we translate it, "It is as you have said." We must be careful not to read the later Johannine account of the interchange between Jesus and Pilate back into this account (cf. John 18:28–40). Each Gospel was written to a particular community, so Matthew's audience would not likely have known the Johannine account. So each account must stand on its own as an interpretation of what happened to Jesus.

There is some evidence that Roman governors could offer an amnesty to someone, perhaps especially at a festival time as a gesture of Roman clemency to those being ruled by Rome. This appears to be what is happening in the account of Barabbas and Jesus being brought before the crowds with the offer of the release of one of them. The account is dripping with irony because Bar-Abba is a name that means "son of the father" in Aramaic, and so the crowd is asked to choose between the false son of the father and the genuine one—and they make the wrong choice. Unlike in the movie *The Passion of the Christ,* we hear of Jesus' flogging by Roman soldiers only briefly and in passing. This is true in all four Gospel accounts. Furthermore, Luke says that the flogging happened as Pilate was trying to release Jesus with a light punishment. What this means is that the flogging was unlikely to have been the extreme flogging with the cat-ó-nine-tails ripping the flesh off of Jesus. Jesus dies of asphyxiation on the cross, as was the case with many another crucifixion victims.

1. What is ironic about the crowd choosing Barabbas over Jesus?

2. What do you make of Pilate? Is he trying to be kind to Jesus, be fair to the judicial process, or avoid giving the Jewish officials what they want?

FOUR

The Death and Burial of Jesus

Matthew 27:45–56 *From noon until three in the afternoon darkness came over all the land.* [46]*About three in the afternoon Jesus cried out in a loud voice, "Eli, Eli, lema sabachthani?" (which means "My God, my God, why have you forsaken me?").*

[47]*When some of those standing there heard this, they said, "He's calling Elijah."*

[48]*Immediately one of them ran and got a sponge. He filled it with wine vinegar, put it on a staff, and offered it to Jesus to drink.* [49]*The rest said, "Now leave him alone. Let's see if Elijah comes to save him."*

[50]*And when Jesus had cried out again in a loud voice, he gave up his spirit.*

[51]*At that moment the curtain of the temple was torn in two from top to bottom. The earth shook, the rocks split* [52]*and the tombs broke open. The bodies of many holy people who had died were raised to life.* [53]*They came out of the tombs after Jesus' resurrection and went into the holy city and appeared to many people.*

[54]*When the centurion and those with him who were guarding Jesus saw the earthquake and all that had happened, they were terrified, and exclaimed, "Surely he was the Son of God!"*

[55]*Many women were there, watching from a distance. They had followed Jesus from Galilee to care for his needs.* [56]*Among them were Mary Magdalene, Mary the mother of James and Joseph, and the mother of Zebedee's sons.*

Key Observation. The events around Jesus' crucifixion signaled that Jesus' death marked the beginning of a new act of God to bring salvation to the world.

Understanding the Word. Let's review the unique elements in the Matthean account. First, there is the witnesses of the crucifixion mistaking "Eli, Eli" for a reference to Elijah when, in fact, it means "my God, my God" as the beginning of the citation of Psalm 22:1. Second, we have the odd story of the opening of the tombs and people going into the city, found only here in this account, and we are told an earthquake caused those tombs to open. Third, the centurion in the Matthean account reacts not just to the way Jesus dies, but to the earthquake which frightens him (cf. Mark 15). Notice, as well, that the centurion is not alone in seeing this and not alone in exclaiming Jesus to be the Son of God. Presumably, we are meant to think that the centurion saw Jesus' death as unjust because, unlike most such victims, Jesus does not rail against God, but dies nobly. Luke has the centurion say, "Surely this was a righteous man" (who didn't deserve to be crucified) (Luke 23:47). The rending of the temple curtain between the holy place and the holy of holies from top to bottom suggests an action of God, perhaps symbolically indicating God's presence leaving the temple.

We have to keep always in mind that crucifixion was the most shameful way to die in antiquity. Nobody viewed it in a positive light. And some even saw it as evidence that a person was cursed by God or the gods. Bear in mind that ancient peoples believed that how a person died most revealed his character, and since no one was looking for a crucified Savior or Messiah, this outcome of the life of Jesus was not expected. If he was such a great miracle worker, why couldn't he just save himself?

Notice that the key witnesses of these events are not the male disciples who have fled the scene, but rather a group of women who had followed Jesus all the way from Galilee (vv. 55–56). Women were last at the cross, first at the tomb on Sunday morning, and first to see Jesus risen from the dead. In a highly patriarchal world, the earliest Christians would never have made up a story about women being the first witnesses to these incredible events. Here we are dealing with historical bedrock for sure, not pious fiction.

1. What is the significance of the three Marys in this passage?

2. What is the meaning of Jesus' crucifixion and the events surrounding it? How do the events of his death signal that something significant has happened?

FIVE

The Resurrection Appearances and the Great Commission

Matthew 28:1–10, 16–20 *After the Sabbath, at dawn on the first day of the week, Mary Magdalene and the other Mary went to look at the tomb.*

[2]There was a violent earthquake, for an angel of the Lord came down from heaven and, going to the tomb, rolled back the stone and sat on it. [3]His appearance was like lightning, and his clothes were white as snow. [4]The guards were so afraid of him that they shook and became like dead men.

[5]The angel said to the women, "Do not be afraid, for I know that you are looking for Jesus, who was crucified. [6]He is not here; he has risen, just as he said. Come and see the place where he lay. [7]Then go quickly and tell his disciples: 'He has risen from the dead and is going ahead of you into Galilee. There you will see him.' Now I have told you."

[8]So the women hurried away from the tomb, afraid yet filled with joy, and ran to tell his disciples. [9]Suddenly Jesus met them. "Greetings," he said. They came to him, clasped his feet and worshiped him. [10]Then Jesus said to them, "Do not be afraid. Go and tell my brothers to go to Galilee; there they will see me." . . .

[16]Then the eleven disciples went to Galilee, to the mountain where Jesus had told them to go. [17]When they saw him, they worshiped him; but some doubted. [18]Then Jesus came to them and said, "All authority in heaven and on earth has been given to me. [19]Therefore go and make disciples of all nations, baptizing them in the name of the Father and of the Son and of the Holy Spirit, [20]and teaching them to obey everything I have commanded you. And surely I am with you always, to the very end of the age."

Key Observation. No one witnessed the resurrection, but Jesus appeared to the women and then to the men in order to reform his community and commission it for mission.

Understanding the Word. The story told in Matthew 28:1–10 is the *Reader's Digest* version of the more detailed account of Jesus' appearance to Mary Magdalene and other women in John 20. Neither the empty tomb nor the angels' message about Jesus was sufficient to create belief in a risen Jesus. Nothing short of actual and physical appearances of Jesus was sufficient to confirm that he was alive again. Resurrection in early Judaism meant the raising of a person into a *physical* body from the grave (see 1 Corinthians 15:12–20 and 35–49, where Paul describes resurrection from out of the realm of the dead). Furthermore, there is a difference in the Greek between "we saw" (which could just be in a vision, as was the case with Paul) and "he appeared." The emphasis is on Jesus' choosing to appear to persons who were not expecting to see him alive when they went to the tomb to complete their mourning of their Master. Resurrection means God's yes to life is even louder than death's no, and it reverses death.

Matthew alone tells the story of the sealing of the tomb and the Roman guards at the tomb. He alone is also the one who tells about the guards' reaction to the angel and the opening of the tomb and then later their report to the authorities. This apologetic motif in Matthew is meant to make clear that Jesus' tomb was not robbed nor was the body moved. Jesus genuinely rose from the dead. Even early Jews who believed in resurrection were not looking for a resurrection of the Messiah, much less his resurrection before the resurrection of all the righteous at the end of day. This narrative conveys the sense of surprise even among the disciples who were forewarned.

The Matthean presentation emphasizes one appearance of Jesus in Jerusalem, though as the Lukan and Johannine accounts show there were more, and one in Galilee, though again, the Johannine account indicates there were more. In Matthew, the first appearance is to the women, then the men are instructed by the women to go meet Jesus in Galilee, and they all go. The astounding thing about that final appearance story is that it says many believed, "but some doubted" (v. 17). They could not even believe their own eyes! This reminds us again that seeing does not necessarily lead to believing, but believing does lead to seeing.

The final unique element in Matthew's Gospel is the Great Commission, which has several key elements: (1) the Father give Jesus all authority in heaven and on earth; (2) Jesus commissions all present, both women and men, to go and make disciples of all the nations ("all" includes Jews and Gentiles outside of the Holy land); (3) the task of making disciples involves both baptism and instruction. Baptism is mentioned first, not second. Baptism was an initiation ritual like circumcision; and (4) the baptism was to be done in the name of the Father, Son, and Spirit, the first reference to Trinitarian baptism. The Gentile nations, however, were being initiated into all the persons of the biblical God since they had no allegiance to any of them before.

Finally, Jesus promises to be with us all until the close of the age, when he will return physically to fully and finally bring the kingdom on earth as it is in heaven. This Immanuel theme found here and in the birth narrative, proclaiming God is with us always, nicely rounds out the Gospel and brings us back to its opening theme.

1. What is the meaning of Jesus' resurrection?

2. How do you participate in Jesus' Great Commission today?

WEEK EIGHT

GATHERING DISCUSSION OUTLINE

A. Open session in prayer. Ask that God would astonish us anew with fresh insight from his Word and transform us into the disciples that Jesus desires us to become.

B. View video for this week's readings.

C. What were key insights or takeaways that you gained from your reading during the week and from watching the video commentary? In particular, how did these help you to grow in your faith and understanding of Scripture? What parts of the Bible lesson or study raised questions for you?

D. Discuss questions selected from the daily readings.

1. KEY OBSERVATION: Understanding the relationship between the cursing of the fig tree and the cleansing of the temple is the key to understanding this passage.

DISCUSSION QUESTION: How does the withering of the fig tree serve as an interpretation of Jesus' actions in the temple?

2. KEY OBSERVATION: Jesus shows that sometimes doing God's will is the opposite of what one wants to do, but submission to God's will is necessary and, in the end, beneficial.

DISCUSSION QUESTION: How does Jesus view his coming death based on what he says at the Last Supper and in the garden?

3. **KEY OBSERVATION:** Although Jesus stood before the Jewish authorities in Matthew 26:57–68, the Roman governor Pilate is the one ultimately responsible for condemning Jesus to death.

   DISCUSSION QUESTION: What do you make of Pilate? Is he trying to be kind to Jesus, be fair to the judicial process, or avoid giving the Jewish officials what they want?

4. **KEY OBSERVATION:** The events around Jesus' crucifixion signaled that Jesus' death marked the beginning of a new act of God to bring salvation to the world.

   DISCUSSION QUESTION: What is the meaning of Jesus' crucifixion and the events surrounding it? How do the events of his death signal that something significant has happened?

5. **KEY OBSERVATION:** No one witnessed the resurrection, but Jesus appeared to the women and then to the men in order to reform his community and commission it for mission.

   DISCUSSION QUESTION: How do you participate in Jesus' Great Commission today?

E. As the study concludes, consider specific ways that this week's Bible lesson invites us to grow and calls us to change. How do this week's scriptures call us to think differently? How do they challenge us to change in order to align ourselves with God's work in the world? What specific actions should we take to apply the insights of the lesson into our daily lives? What kind of person does our Bible lesson call us to become?

F. Close session with prayer. Emphasize God's ongoing work of transformation in our lives in preparation for loving mission and service in the world. Pray for missing class members as well as for persons whom we need to invite to join our study.

CPSIA information can be obtained
at www.ICGtesting.com
Printed in the USA
LVHW030818070720
659956LV00007B/10

9 781628 240627